NEW DIRECTIONS FOR INSTITUTIONAL RESEARCH

Patrick T. Terenzini, *The Pennsylvania State University*
EDITOR-IN-CHIEF

J. Fredericks Volkwein, *State University of New York at Albany*
EDITOR-ELECT

Student Tracking: New Techniques, New Demands

Peter T. Ewell
National Center for Higher Education Management Systems

EDITOR

Number 87, Fall 1995

JOSSEY-BASS PUBLISHERS
San Francisco

STUDENT TRACKING: NEW TECHNIQUES, NEW DEMANDS
Peter T. Ewell (ed.)
New Directions for Institutional Research, no. 87
Volume XVII, Number 3
Patrick T. Terenzini, Editor-in-Chief

Microfilm copies of issues and articles are available in 16mm and 35mm, as well as microfiche in 105mm, through University Microfilms Inc., 300 North Zeeb Road, Ann Arbor, Michigan 48106-1346.

LC 85-645339   ISSN 0271-0579   ISBN 0-7879-9943-1

NEW DIRECTIONS FOR INSTITUTIONAL RESEARCH is part of The Jossey-Bass Higher and Adult Education Series and is published quarterly by Jossey-Bass Inc., Publishers, 350 Sansome Street, San Francisco, California 94104-1342 (publication number USPS 098-830). Second-class postage paid at San Francisco, California, and at additional mailing offices. POST-MASTER: Send address changes to New Directions for Institutional Research, Jossey-Bass Inc., Publishers, 350 Sansome Street, San Francisco, California 94104-1342.

SUBSCRIPTIONS for 1995 cost $48.00 for individuals and $64.00 for institutions, agencies, and libraries.

EDITORIAL CORRESPONDENCE should be sent to editor-elect J. Fredericks Volkwein, Institutional Research, Administration 241, State University of New York at Albany, Albany, NY 12222.

Manufactured in the United States of America on Lyons Falls Pathfinder Tradebook. This paper is acid-free and 100 percent totally chlorine-free.

ORDERING INFORMATION

NEW DIRECTIONS FOR INSTITUTIONAL RESEARCH is a series of paperback books that provides planners and administrators in all types of academic institutions with guidelines in such areas as resource coordination, information analysis, program evaluation, and institutional management. Books in the series are published quarterly in spring, summer, fall, and winter and are available for purchase by subscription as well as by single copy.

SUBSCRIPTIONS for 1995 cost $48.00 for individuals (a savings of 29 percent over single-copy prices) and $64.00 for institutions, agencies, and libraries. Please do not send institutional checks for personal subscriptions. Standing orders are accepted.

SINGLE COPIES cost $19.00 plus shipping (see below) when payment accompanies order. California, New Jersey, New York, and Washington, D.C., residents please include appropriate sales tax. Canadian residents add GST and any local taxes. Billed orders will be charged shipping and handling. No billed shipments to post office boxes. Orders from outside the United States or Canada *must be prepaid* in U.S. dollars or charged to VISA, MasterCard, or American Express.

SHIPPING (SINGLE COPIES ONLY): one issue, add $3.50; two issues, add $4.50; three issues, add $5.50; four to five issues, add $6.50; six to seven issues, add $7.50; eight or more issues, add $8.50.

DISCOUNTS FOR QUANTITY ORDERS are available. Please write to the address below for information.

ALL ORDERS must include either the name of an individual or an official purchase order number. Please submit your order as follows:
    Subscriptions: specify series and year subscription is to begin
    Single copies: include individual title code (such as IR78)

MAIL ALL ORDERS TO:
    Jossey-Bass Publishers
    350 Sansome Street
    San Francisco, CA 94104-1342

FOR SUBSCRIPTION SALES OUTSIDE OF THE UNITED STATES, CONTACT: any international subscription agency or Jossey-Bass directly.

CONTENTS

EDITOR'S NOTES

Longitudinal student tracking systems, developed originally to support research on retention, must now serve a multitude of masters. Information needed to meet growing accountability demands from states, accrediting bodies, and the federal government prominently features such measures as persistence, graduation, and time-to-degree. Required measures of performance are increasingly reaching beyond enrollment at a particular institution to address such matters as occupational placement, licensure passage, or interinstitutional transfer.

At the same time, resource shortfalls are driving both institutions and state systems to examine their operations more carefully to achieve greater coherence and efficiency; understanding and monitoring student flow is a prominent part of this effort. At the institutional level, this may mean moving beyond simple retention calculations to investigate the optimal patterns of course taking needed to minimize time-to-degree, or the effectiveness of established placement policies or basic-skills instructional programs for particular types of students. At the state system level, it implies paying far more attention to empirical patterns of articulation and transfer among institutions.

Finally, technical developments have opened up new possibilities for conducting student tracking studies. On one hand, data bases beyond the boundaries of the individual campuses are becoming more accessible in such areas as K–12 experiences, employment, and further education. On the other, quantum leaps in computing power and capacity allow the development of far more flexible approaches to defining, building, and manipulating longitudinal data files.

In the face of these developments, student tracking has come of age. The purpose of this volume is to characterize this new maturity by describing important changes in context over the past decade that have a direct impact on the demand for and construction of longitudinal data bases, examining new technical opportunities in the realm of available data bases and data-manipulation tools for constructing and analyzing longitudinal data, and providing practical advice to institutional researchers about how to respond to these developments.

Logic of Student Tracking

The basic concepts underlying student tracking are comparatively simple and despite considerable technical progress have changed little over the past three decades. The logic of tracking rests first on identification of a particular tracking cohort, all members of which meet a set of common conditions at the point at which tracking begins. The most common such condition, and the

NEW DIRECTIONS FOR INSTITUTIONAL RESEARCH, no. 87, Fall 1995 © Jossey-Bass Publishers

one fundamental to calculating uniform graduation and persistence statistics, is that of entering the institution for the first time in a particular term. The institutional tracking cohort most often in use at most institutions consists of all degree-seeking students entering the institution as full-time, first-time students in a particular fall term, although many alternative cohort definitions are possible and may be appropriate for various purposes. At the state level, for example, it is often useful to construct alternative cohorts on the basis of when a student first enters the state system of higher education by enrolling at any institution, in order to track patterns of interinstitutional migration. Within institutions, moreover, appropriate alternative cohorts might be constructed for newly entering transfer students, or on the basis of when a student entered a particular major or exited a particular course, regardless of when he or she first entered the institution. The objective of any cohort definition, in short, is to establish a common starting point that provides a baseline against which to compare patterns of enrollment or performance over time.

Once assigned to a particular cohort for the purposes of an analysis, a student remains a member of that cohort for the duration of that analysis. Data elements are then assembled reflecting the condition or behavior of each student as of particular points in time. At the most elementary level, for example, the resulting record might contain a set of demographic descriptors for each student in the cohort, followed by a set of data elements containing the number of credits enrolled for and completed by that student in each subsequent term of enrollment, together with information about whether and when the student graduated. Compiled for a full-time, first-time entering cohort of students, even this rudimentary longitudinal file allows a range of persistence and graduation-rate statistics to be compiled for different types of students, and would thus allow an institution to respond initially to most external reporting requirements. At the most sophisticated levels, a range of student descriptors might be assembled for each student, including pre-enrollment characteristics drawn from high school or previous college records, selected experiences while enrolled such as particular courses taken or services received (such as counselling or financial aid), and academic or behavioral outcomes such as credentials earned, academic standing, and the results of any specially constructed assessments. Such a data file might be useful in supporting a broad range of internal studies about the effectiveness of particular interventions or the effects of particular enrollment experiences on later performance.

Though simple in concept, constructing and working with longitudinal files poses a number of operational challenges. First, to be meaningful, all cohort data must be assembled and analyzed on a specific point-in-time basis. For example, if an analysis of the impact of changing majors on students' time-to-graduation is contemplated, data elements on all the majors that each student historically enrolled in, and the times that any changes in major occurred, will be required. Obtaining such information retrospectively from a typical transaction-oriented student record system may be difficult because most such systems routinely overwrite old values of data elements such as academic major with more current information as a student's status changes. This situation becomes more complicated when other phenomena of interest begin to be examined, such as whether a student retook a particular class for a better grade, or received and later made up a substantial number of incomplete grades. A first important tracking operation, then, is to accomplish the necessary point-in-time extracts required to assemble an accurate picture of each student's status during each portion of the cohort's history.

Complicating things further is the fact that the data elements of interest for a given longitudinal analysis rarely are stored in the same subfiles of a student records system. Over time, moreover, they are generally located in discrete term files that may or may not be on-line simultaneously. To accomplish a longitudinal analysis at all, data on a given student must be linked across several terms of academic history, using a student identification number as a linking element. For more sophisticated analyses, additional information on academic experiences and outcomes after college (such as job placement) must be similarly linked into each student's record. Efficiently merging data elements drawn from a range of original source data bases thus constitutes a second important tracking operation, and one that depends decisively on the presence of adequate key links, such as student identifiers or Social Security numbers, in all the base records from which data are to be drawn.

Moreover, the data elements typically included in a longitudinal study rarely provide much usable information in themselves. Unlike cross-sectional enrollment analyses that primarily involve counting students by category, meaningful longitudinal statistics almost always depend on constructed ratios or other more sophisticated manipulations of base data elements. Calculating graduation or placement rates, for instance, requires the application of both a set of selection criteria that govern the inclusion of students in the numerator and the denominator, and a set of rules that govern the calculation of the rate itself. Similarly, establishing the efficacy of a given pattern of coursework or intervention requires recalculating such rates for different student subpopulations experiencing and not experiencing this pattern. A third important tracking operation, therefore, is recoding and data manipulation to produce analytical variables of interest, once a longitudinal record for a given cohort has been established.

Finally, because they are unfamiliar to decision makers, the results of longitudinal analyses present unusual challenges for reporting. Except under the most traditional collegiate conditions in which all students begin as first-year students in a given fall term, entering cohorts rarely correspond to any student groupings with which administrators are familiar. Furthermore, the performance statistics of interest are almost always derived and may require a great deal of accompanying explanation. Considerable care is therefore needed in a fourth principal tracking operation: reporting results in a manner accessible to and usable by decision makers.

The technical and analytical requirements for accomplishing each of these four basic tracking operations often differ substantially. This is the principal reason why the straightforward set of concepts underlying student tracking has so often encountered operational difficulty.

Organization of the Volume

As the chapters in this volume illustrate, many of the difficulties noted above are now being overcome at the same time as new data sources are coming on-line that can extend substantially the coverage of the resulting data bases. In order to explore this growing potential, a first section of the volume provides a perspective on the historical development of student tracking methodology and its current practice in institutional and state settings. In Chapter One, I examine the evolution of tracking design and the current demands for information about student progress and performance that any tracking system must be designed to meet. The next three chapters provide examples of evolving practice within this context. In Chapter Two, John Porter and Melinda Gebel describe the practice of tracking in a four-year university context, emphasizing particularly the ways in which several general-purpose longitudinal data bases were developed to meet different analytical needs. Stanley Adelman takes up the story by providing an engaging account of the development and operation of a tracking capability in a community college context, focusing specifically on the salient need in this context to examine the effectiveness of remedial study. Both are nuts-and-bolts presentations that reflect both consistent good sense and the application of evolving technologies. Finally, Alene Russell and Mark Chisholm examine the same topic from a state perspective and present data drawn from a newly completed survey of state-level student tracking capabilities.

The volume's second section explores some emerging frontiers. Victor Borden in Chapter Five provides a succinct review of important changes in the technical environment and highlights the ways these new directions will increasingly allow longitudinal analyses to be conducted more flexibly and efficiently. The next two chapters describe additional data sources that enable researchers to investigate student performance after leaving a given institution. In Chapter Six, Michael Green examines the growing potential of electronic transcript exchange as an alternative to transfer follow-up studies in obtaining information about the performance of students at other institutions. In Chapter Seven, Loretta Seppanen provides an analysis of the promise and pitfalls of using wage-record and other administrative data bases as an approach to determining vocational placement and career success. Special thanks are due to Jay Pfeiffer of the Florida Education and Training Placement Information Program and to David Stevens of the University of Baltimore for their help with this chapter. An Additional Resources section is included at the end of the volume for the reader to obtain further information.

Based on these analyses and experiences, I attempt in the final chapter to draw some appropriate implications for institutional research practice. Although some of these implications are driven by emerging technical opportunities, others are based on enduring principles first established by those engaged in longitudinal work many years ago. All reflect the fact that even after more than three decades of practice, the examination of student performance over time remains as much art as science, and despite undeniable technical progress, will no doubt continue to do so.

Peter T. Ewell
Editor

PETER T. EWELL *is senior associate at the National Center for Higher Education Management Systems in Boulder, Colorado.*

Student tracking approaches have been shaped by changing contexts and evolving technical capabilities. Institutional researchers should know this history and be aware of the specific demands for information that future tracking systems must meet.

Working over Time: The Evolution of Longitudinal Student Tracking Data Bases

Peter T. Ewell

Student tracking methodologies, like other institutional research tools, have been decisively shaped by both available technologies and changing informational demands. The result has been considerable technical evolution as well as the vindication of some time-tested principles. This chapter helps set the stage for this issue by examining both. The first section provides a brief historical review of the specific demands and opportunities that have conditioned the development of longitudinal data bases over the past three decades. More to the point, it notes important areas in which these background conditions have changed. The second section summarizes the specific demands that in today's context any student tracking system must be designed to meet.

Evolution of Tracking System Design

Since their emergence four decades ago, longitudinal student data bases have evolved in response to three quite different informational requirements. The first such tools were designed specifically to support research about student development in college and had little direct application to institutional research. The data files assembled by higher education scholars quickly proved useful in meeting a growing need for institution-specific information about student retention and the effectiveness of particular programs and policies. This yielded a second, quite different informational demand—to inform institutional planning, evaluation, and decision making—that has grown significantly as enrollment behavior has become more complex. A third such demand was external: rapid expansion in government reporting requirements throughout the 1980s. Such mandates now commonly require institutions to provide data on completion rates, time-to-degree, job placement, and the effectiveness of interinstitutional articulation, in addition to standard cross-sectional enrollment reporting.

Each of these three demands has exerted a unique influence on data base design, and to some extent they arose in sequence. At the same time, steady progress in available computing technology allowed new features to be continuously incorporated into existing approaches. The result has been three distinct stages of design evolution in student tracking's brief history.

Retention Scholarship: The Handicraft Era of Design. Beginning in the mid 1960s, there was a veritable explosion of research about college attrition. This was partly because the subject was topical as college attendance expanded. Equally compelling from the point of view of scholarship because of its unambiguous dependent variable and its amenability to causal modeling, the study of dropout behavior provided a proving ground on which to deploy a growing array of empirical weapons from the arsenals of social science. By the mid 1970s, several hundred studies had been conducted and the field was ripe for theoretical synthesis (Spady, 1971; Tinto, 1975). The result was an unusually powerful set of conceptual models based on constructs such as involvement (Astin, 1975, 1993) and academic and social integration (Tinto, 1975, 1987) that eventually proved useful across a wide range of student behaviors (Pascarella and Terenzini, 1991).

Making good use of these constructs required both definitional clarity about key terms and far better data about college conditions and behaviors. The first challenge was met promptly, and by the early 1980s considerable consensus about core concepts had been reached (Lenning, Beal, and Sauer, 1980). The second problem was more difficult to address. Researchers quickly came to the conclusion that systematic, long-term, longitudinal studies conducted on a cohort basis were required. Neither cross-sectional "snapshots" of experiences collected from mixed samples of students at different stages in their academic careers nor "autopsy" designs that followed up dropouts after withdrawal could provide the levels of statistical control needed to reliably investigate influences on enrollment behaviors (Terenzini, 1987; Tinto, 1975).

In fact, the longitudinal data sets needed to support such work had to meet some very rigorous design criteria. First, they had to include a large number of variables of quite different kinds. Initially, these included student demographic and educational background characteristics, academic choices and experiences such as enrolling in a particular major, and collegiate academic performance—information generally available through existing transcript records. The resulting data bases were quite limited analytically, however, because they lacked information about the factors thought to be most powerfully related to attrition. As a result, data on student perceptions, goals, and academic and social experiences—collected by questionnaire at multiple points in a cohort's history—quickly came to be included. Adding such variables contributed much to the research utility of the resulting data files, but both expense and logistics generally precluded collecting them for all students on a routine basis.

A second design requirement for such data bases was that they be constructed in a format that allowed the necessary statistical analyses to be conducted. At the time, this meant that they had to be organized as collections of single, fixed-length data records—a requisite (since relaxed) of the major software packages then capable of conducting complex, multivariate statistical analyses (Endo and Bittner, 1985). Merging the necessary data elements into a single record was often an extremely labor-intensive activity. Because of this, carefully selected samples of students rather the entire population were often used.

Methodologies of this kind supported the majority of foundation studies of student attrition and college impact and remained dominant through the late 1970s. The resulting longitudinal data files allowed powerful analyses to be conducted, but once assembled, they were relatively inflexible. Crafted individually to meet the demands of a particular research design and often highly restricted in scope, they were thus rarely applicable to broader institutional research purposes.

Tracking Data Bases: The Industrial Design Phase. As long as a majority of students attended college in the traditional full-time, four-year pattern, the study of attrition remained principally of scholarly interest. By the mid 1970s, however, projected shortfalls in traditional-age students had institutional administrators worried. Pressures on enrollments forced greater attention to recruiting nontraditional students and increasing retention rates. As student bodies became more diverse, so did their patterns of attendance. Both phenomena began affecting institutional revenue streams, either through lost tuition or forgone state reimbursements granted on a full-time-equivalent basis. As a consequence, obtaining institution-specific information about student progress became more important for internal planning and decision making. At the same time, rising public accountability concerns throughout the 1980s drove a new set of external reporting requirements, increasingly centered on graduation rates and time-to-degree.

Institutional interest in obtaining student persistence data outside the realm of scholarship arose in two main areas, each of which quickly became important topics for institutional research. The first was largely technical and concerned the projection of future enrollments. Faced with quite different patterns of student progression, traditional enrollment projection methods based on incremental averaging tended to break down (Wing, 1974). Cohort-based methods founded on actual data about the continuation patterns of particular student subpopulations, though far more difficult to apply, proved considerably more accurate. A second area of application was programmatic. With institutional revenue at stake, comprehensive institutional retention programs began to emerge, focused mainly on coordinating action among the many offices and programs designed to help students succeed (Kemmerer, Baldridge, and Green, 1982). By the mid 1980s, under the label *enrollment management* (Hossler, 1984; Hossler, Bean, and Associates, 1990), comprehensive approaches of this kind were well-established and demanded considerable data to support them (Ewell, 1987).

Meanwhile, external interest in reporting data about student progress had also arisen for several reasons. First, court-ordered efforts to desegregate public higher education in the southeast in the 1960s and early 1970s focused considerable attention on the performance of minority college students. As a result, consistent reporting of black persistence and graduation rates to the federal Office of Civil Rights became a prominent feature of the consent decrees signed by the so-called Adams States during this period. Though limited in scope, these requirements placed enormous demands on existing institutional record-keeping capabilities and helped to stimulate interest in creating the first systematic institutional tracking systems and the nation's first statewide unit-record reporting systems. Similarly, as reported abuses in college athletics became prominent, parallel interest in the graduation performance of student athletes arose. Resulting reporting requirements of the National Collegiate Athletic Association (NCAA) have been in place since 1986 for institutions offering athletic aid (Mallette and Howard, 1992). These requirements also encouraged institutions to develop an initial tracking capability.

Following these leads, a new wave of reporting requirements of far wider scope began to emerge. By the end of the 1980s, a majority of states had enacted assessment mandates requiring public institutions to regularly report retention and graduation rates together with other statistics on institutional performance (Ewell, 1991). At the same time, student graduation and persistence rates became increasingly prominent in the self-studies typically produced for both regional and professional accreditation. Culminating this period in 1990 was the Student Right-to-Know and Campus Security Act, a measure that required all institutions, public and private, to report graduation rates as a condition of continued participation in federal student aid programs.

Growing institutional demands for planning information, combined with escalating reporting requirements, yielded the classic free-standing, cohort-based student tracking model now in place at many institutions (Clagget, 1992; Middaugh, 1992; Ewell, Parker, and Jones, 1988). Although based on the longitudinal logic of earlier attrition-research data bases, three specific features of this approach reflect additional needs to produce readily interpretable information on a consistent basis. First, data elements included in such systems are typically extracted directly from regular institutional operating data bases such as registration and admissions. Once the programming needed to accomplish the extraction is in place, these routines are run each term as part of the institution's standard data-processing schedule. In this way, data can be easily assembled for all applicable students, not just a sample. Second, the physical structure of the data base—a set of fixed data elements reflecting student background and incoming characteristics, followed by successive term blocks of behavioral and performance data elements arrayed in comparable form for each potential term of enrollment—enables data to be readily read and analyzed by statistical software packages such as SAS and SPSS. Finally, use of the table-generation capabilities of such software packages allows standard preprogrammed cohort progression and performance reports to be constructed that can be run for any designated subpopulation of students. This feature offers considerable analytical power while still allowing relatively nontechnical users to manipulate the data file.

Since its emergence in the early 1980s, this longitudinal data base design has proven robust over a wide range of settings, and it remains for most institutions the standard. However, this design has notable drawbacks. Probably the most important is its basic inflexibility. Because the organizing principle is a particular incoming cohort, the entire file must be rebuilt if the definition of a cohort changes. Although this poses few drawbacks for "official" student reporting, it makes it awkward to track students based on alternative startpoints of interest after initial enrollment (such as all students exiting from remedial activity in the same term or all those becoming chemistry majors at a particular time). A second, less serious drawback is the fact that the specific data content of free-standing tracking files tends by nature to be limited, especially in the realm of term-tracking elements that must occur repeatedly. The larger the number of data elements included in such files, the greater the need to maintain complex extract programs and the greater the processing time required to conduct an analysis. As a result, many variables of potential interest are excluded from such files and must be merged into them on an ad hoc basis. Not only is this an additional step, but it also may require considerable technical expertise to accomplish effectively.

Fully Relational Data Bases: A Postindustrial Design Phase? Experience with the free-standing cohort tracking file forms the basis of chapters Two and Three of this issue. As illustrated by these two case studies, moreover, this approach has undergone considerable technical evolution within the same basic structure. Although it was initially implemented on mainframe computers using SAS or SPSS, the increasing power and flexibility of microcomputer data bases and statistical packages have led growing numbers of institutions to adopt this environment. Continuing experience with increasingly powerful processors and the relational data base structures that they support also allows researchers to move beyond the free-standing tracking file entirely.

As suggested in Chapter Five, the classic tracking model of the 1980s was always a design compromise. Few computing environments then allowed a user to access a large number of base record files—such as those associated with successive terms—at the same time. The tracking data base approach allowed such a record to be assembled one step at a time, archiving the result of each step for later retrieval and analysis, but at the considerable price of later inability to modify its structure and contents. Order-of-magnitude increases in available workspace, together with the ability of current data base software to quickly link data elements drawn from a wide range of disparate sources, promise to overcome this limitation.

At the same time, this new technology makes it far more feasible to incorporate data of the kinds covered in chapters Six and Seven that allow tracking of student experience beyond a particular campus. First, such information simply is more accessible. As indicated in Chapter Four, state-level unit-record data bases covering public institutions are now in place or planned in thirty-five states, potentially allowing access to enrollment records throughout a given state or system. Increasingly, moreover, states in the same region are allowing access to one another's files on a limited basis to facilitate such tracking. As discussed in Chapter Seven, additional data bases such as unemployment insurance wage records and military personnel records are being made available to researchers investigating such topics as workforce placement and return on investment. Using such data bases effectively, however, requires a very high level of computing power and flexibility. The growing availability of sophisticated data manipulation software thus also allows users to access and merge selected data elements drawn from individual records in such data bases with institutional enrollment records, matched by a social security number (or other linking identifier).

Current and Anticipated Demands for Information

Given this changing history, what kinds of information on student progress and performance are needed to cope with the management and accountability environment of the 1990s? As in the past, a first set of requirements is driven by internal institutional imperatives. However, institutional requirements for information these days are driven primarily by demands to do more with less and to serve an expanding and increasingly diverse student population. A second set of external demands remains focused on accountability but is additionally characterized by a new rhetoric of consumer protection, institutional quality assurance, and funding for results. In short, the stakes are much higher today than when student tracking models first emerged, and their use is likely to become increasingly central.

Internal Demand for Information: Evaluation, Restructuring, and Continuous Improvement. Even at "traditional" institutions, few students now fit the model of four-year single-institution attendance largely assumed by the classic retention studies of the 1960s and 1970s. Many take more than four years to complete their programs because of part-time attendance or stop-out, or attend multiple institutions before earning a degree. Others shift programs repeatedly while enrolled, losing credits in the process, which may delay their graduation; some cannot obtain the classes they need in order to graduate on time. Finally, increasing numbers arrive with academic deficiencies that require remediation, which not only increases time-to-completion but raises additional questions about the effectiveness of such programs and the efficacy of the criteria used to place students in them. In the face of this complexity, a first requirement is descriptive. Whatever design is chosen, the resulting data base must be capable of succinctly disaggregating patterns of student flow in a manner that indicates which kinds of students are experiencing these patterns under what conditions.

With the changing student population has come a bewildering variety of instruction and service delivery modes. On the instructional front, modular (non-term-based) coursework, distance and computer-assisted delivery, and self-paced programs have become increasingly common as institutions seek alternative ways to serve larger numbers of students more effectively and cheaply. At the same time, many institutions now offer a broad array of specially designed support programs to serve particular student populations or to provide particular services. Moreover, institutions rarely replace existing activities with new alternatives; these are usually layered onto existing courses and programs. A second demand for longitudinal analysis, therefore, is to provide concrete evaluative evidence about which kinds of programs appear to work best for which kinds of students.

Finally, the fiscal environment in which all of this is happening is increasingly constrained. This is one reason for unprecedented levels of experimentation in instructional delivery intended to provide equivalent educational experiences at decreased cost. For the same reason, growing numbers of institutions are exploring ways to restructure their curricula and academic support programs to gain greater coherence and achieve higher levels of productivity. Much of this activity is occurring under the rubric of continuous quality improvement—higher education's own version of the total quality management techniques drawn originally from business and industry (Sherr and Teeter, 1991). These approaches are at their best when they are applied to complex processes of linked components that operate in sequence to produce a particular outcome—precisely what a curriculum is supposed to do (Ewell, 1992). A third demand for longitudinal analysis, then, is to ground institutional investigations of how existing student course-taking patterns might be streamlined or how students might complete the same requirements in shorter periods of time.

One way to summarize the collective impact of these demands for longitudinal information is to pose some of the specific questions that future tracking systems must answer. Among them are the following:

• How do patterns of persistence vary from year to year among different gender and ethnic combinations? During which terms of enrollment, for instance, do the largest numbers of black male students drop out? Are there differences in the apparent reasons for withdrawal at different points? For example, do students who drop out early in the tracking period tend to do so in good standing, or with failing grades? Although such information is basically descriptive, it will be of considerable administrative value in understanding the dynamics of enrollment.

• Are there a limited number (four or five) modal patterns of longitudinal enrollment that account for the vast majority of student experience? For instance, does one group of students principally attend full-time until earning a degree, another stop out after two or three terms then re-enroll a year later, another attend only winter terms, another attend only the first year and never return? What are the specific demographic and academic characteristics of each of these quite distinctive student bodies? Information of this kind may be useful not only as an overview of enrollment dynamics, but also in the development and assessment of program initiatives tailored to meet the needs of each of these "behavioral populations."

• Do students engaging in different kinds of remedial math programs (such as course-based, self-paced, or math lab) experience different success rates in the first college-level algebra course they enroll in? Do success rates for the students experiencing each mode of delivery appear to be related to any prior student characteristics? For instance, does one method appear to work better for minority students than another? How do these rates compare to their counterparts for students who never needed remediation in math? Information of this kind is critical for assessing program effectiveness and to help make decisions about where to invest scarce resources.

• Does frequency of contact with particular student service or academic support offices (such as the women's counseling center) appear to have an impact on persistence and ultimate graduation for the students targeted by these programs? What other factors appear to be associated with any gains experienced, and how do these gains (if any) compare to the costs of continuing to run such intervention programs? Again, information here is principally directed toward program evaluation and cost-effectiveness.

• What specific factors appear to be responsible for students taking longer than expected to complete their academic programs? For instance, how much impact does changing majors seem to have? Attending part-time or stopping out? Enrolling for additional credits that are not required for graduation, or re-taking courses for improvements in grades? Which of these factors appear to be institutional factors that might be addressed through policy, and which are matters of individual student choice over which the institution has little control? Information of this kind is needed to help design new academic policies that enable students to graduate more quickly.

• How many and which types of students appear to be violating current academic policies or prerequisites, and with what consequences for later success? Based on the experience of these students, are these policies or prerequisites really needed? This information is useful in re-examining current operations to achieve greater efficiencies.

The ability to answer questions such as these requires an established institutional tracking capability that is extremely flexible. Especially salient under these conditions is the ability to quickly and efficiently link together data elements drawn from a variety of sources, including standard institutional records at a high level of transcript detail and the results of special data-collection efforts such as assessment. Equally compelling is the need to quickly disaggregate performance information for different student populations and display the results in a manner that is readily accessible to decision makers.

External Demand for Information: Comparative Performance and Consumer Protection. Responding effectively to external demands for information about student performance will increasingly demand equivalent flexibility. The most insistent of these demands, of course, remains centered on rates of graduation and program completion. More than a third of the states now require public colleges and universities to regularly calculate and report such statistics as part of newly established performance indicator systems intended to improve accountability (Ruppert, 1994). Driven largely by concerns about efficiency, these systems often include additional longitudinal performance measures such as time-to-degree or the proportion of regular students finishing within a traditional two- or four-year time frame. Significantly, such measures are also becoming part of increasingly popular state performance-funding approaches, where specific levels of performance on the part of institutions—or demonstrated improvements in performance—are rewarded through the allocation of additional set-aside funds (Ewell, 1994).

Meanwhile, anticipated implementation of the controversial Student Right-to-Know and Campus Security Act (many times delayed) has both stimulated and standardized graduation-rate reporting. Following the methodology established by this legislation, virtually all established state-level reporting schemes track full-time first-time degree-seeking students entering in a given fall term, and calculate graduation rates as a proportion of this group completing programs within 150 percent of catalogue program length. This method is the one proposed by the National Center for Education Statistics, which plans to incorporate graduation-rate reporting into regular Integrated Postsecondary Educational Data System institutional enrollment reporting cycles within the next five years. The nomenclature and construction of student right-to-know requirements signalled a new public sensitivity toward consumer protection. Similar concerns have emerged at the state level, and show few signs of abating. As a result, growing numbers of state-level longitudinal reporting statistics are being constructed from the student's standpoint, emphasizing, for instance, the chances of success that newly enrolled students of varying types might reasonably expect if they enroll in a particular institution or program.

A second prominent theme is associated with growing concerns about program effectiveness, especially in the realm of remedial or developmental education. The multi-institutional Longitudinal Evaluation Student Tracking and Reporting (LONESTAR) system developed in Texas in the late 1980s, for instance, was directly stimulated by legislation requiring public institutions to report on the performance of remediated students in later college-level work, and to feed back information on college performance to high schools (Adelman, Ewell, and Grable, 1989). Similar remedial tracking and feedback-reporting requirements are in place in many states, often operating as part of a more comprehensive state assessment mandate. Value-added assessment designs involving examination of the test–retest performance of designated groups of students over time have also been widely stimulated by such mandates and similarly require good longitudinal data on student enrollment behavior to be effective (Astin, 1991).

A third growing emphasis of public reporting—student outcomes after graduation—is consistent with both rising concerns about program effectiveness and growing demands for consumer information. Most state-level graduation-reporting schemes recognize that successful transfer to another institution at a higher level may constitute an alternative form of completion, especially in the two-year college environment. Similarly, reporting requirements associated with vocational programs at both the state and federal levels increasingly center on such outcomes as subsequent job placement or success in passing applicable certification or licensure requirements. Continuing participation in federal Carl Perkins vocational programs, for example, requires each state to set appropriate standards and measures embracing such matters; partly as a result, Carl Perkins funds have been used to support the development of multi- institutional student-tracking efforts in a number of states.

Given these often quite different concerns, the specific types of questions posed by external bodies that future student tracking capabilities must meet include the following:

• What is the overall six-year completion rate for students who received state financial aid in their first year of enrollment, versus those who received no aid? What proportion of entering full-time baccalaureate-seeking students completed their programs in four years? What were the specific characteristics of those who did not? Information of this kind is typical of the growing sophistication in required reporting that is now emerging at the state level.

• Based on past history, what are the chances that an entering Hispanic male student with a high-school grade-point average of less than 2.5 will, on entering the institution be placed in a remedial program, successfully pass out of that program, survive his first year of enrollment, eventually complete a degree program, and obtain employment in a field related to that program as a result? How long will he typically take to complete the program? Statistics of this kind are consistent with an emerging emphasis on consumer disclosure now apparent in public reporting.

• What proportion of entering students who are placed in the most basic level of math remediation eventually register for a collegiate-level math course? At what level of entering student ability does the proportion successfully completing a collegiate-level math course exceed 50 percent? Information of this kind is increasingly in demand from state authorities to make pipeline decisions about whether entrance to postsecondary study should be restricted to those with an ability to benefit.

• What proportion of students entering a four-year institution for the first time had previous postsecondary experience at a two-year institution, and how did such students perform with respect to degree-completion and proportion of upper-division courses passed? Such questions are typical of those associated with statewide articulation policy as the frequency of students attending multiple institutions continues to grow.

• What proportion of students enrolling in vocational programs obtain related employment, within what time period, and at what salary levels? Does the money they make allow them to quickly recover their costs of attendance and the income forgone during school? Information of this kind is typical of the growing number of return-on-investment questions now being asked about vocational and professional programs by both state and federal agencies.

As in the internal domain, effectively answering such questions demands tracking capabilities that are comprehensive and flexible. Comprehensiveness is needed because statistics about the performance of growing numbers of special student populations are needed, and the definitions of exactly who is to be included in such populations are often unpredictable. As specially funded government programs tailored to meet the needs of particular types of students have proliferated, so have demands for information about their performance, and each program often defines performance in a different way. Building the institutional procedures needed to respond to each of these requirements individually or in different offices within the institution—as has generally been attempted in the past—is simply no longer feasible (Ewell and Jones, 1991). Flexibility is needed because reporting requirements of this kind will continue to evolve in a piecemeal fashion, probably at faster rates than before. Despite considerable behavioral convergence, for instance, there is no established national definition of how to calculate a completion rate. As a result, the statistics required by state governments, civil rights or "special populations" offices, and organizations such as the NCAA remain exasperatingly diverse.

Given these conditions, institutions will also increasingly need analytical approaches capable of producing the required performance statistics quickly, without continually re-engineering analytical data files and statistical calculation routines. Above all in this evolving accountability environment, institutions will need the ability to quickly reanalyze or rebut statistics that are inappropriately reported by public bodies or the media. Tracking systems that are simply able to generate the required reporting statistics, without being able to produce additional contextual information that might address why particular outcomes occurred as they did or to produce data on the student populations that did well or badly, will significantly handicap institutions in responding to a volatile high-stakes accountability context.

Meeting these emerging demands will be challenging for institutional researchers, and many have already felt the burdens of "working over time." But both new technologies and established experience also promise to make the next decade of student tracking one of increased sophistication.

References

Adelman, S. I., Ewell, P. T., and Grable, J. R. "LONESTAR: Texas's Voluntary Tracking and Developmental Education Evaluation System." In T. H. Bers (ed.), *Using Student Tracking Systems Effectively*. New Directions for Community Colleges, no. 66. San Francisco: Jossey-Bass, 1989.

Astin, A. W. *Preventing Students from Dropping Out.* San Francisco: Jossey-Bass, 1975.

Astin, A. W. *Assessment for Excellence: The Philosophy and Practice of Assessment and Evaluation in Higher Education.* New York: Macmillan, 1991.

Astin, A. W. *What Matters in College: Four Critical Years Revisited.* San Francisco: Jossey-Bass, 1993.

Clagget, C. "Enrollment Management." In M. A. Whiteley, J. D. Porter, and R. H. Fenske (eds.), *The Primer for Institutional Research.* Tallahassee, Fla.: Association for Institutional Research, 1992, pp. 12–24.

Endo, J., and Bittner, T. "Developing and Using a Longitudinal Student Outcomes Data File: The University of Colorado Experience." In P. T. Ewell (ed.), *Assessing Educational Outcomes.* New Directions in Institutional Research, no. 47. San Francisco: Jossey-Bass, 1985.

Ewell, P. T. "Principles of Longitudinal Enrollment Analysis: Conducting Retention and Student Flow Studies." In J. A. Muffo and G. W. McLaughlin (eds.), *A Primer on Institutional Research.* Tallahassee, Fla.: Association for Institutional Research, 1987.

Ewell, P. T. "Assessment and Accountability: Back to the Future." *Change,* Nov./Dec. 1991, 23 (6) 12–17.

Ewell, P. T. "Longitudinal Databases: A Critical Tool for Managing Quality in Higher Education." In J. W. Harris and J. M. Baggett (eds.), *Quality Quest in the Academic Process.* Birmingham, Ala.: Samford University, 1992.

Ewell, P. T. "Developing Statewide Performance Indicators for Higher Education: Policy Themes and Variations." In S. Ruppert (ed.), *Charting Higher Education Accountability: A Sourcebook on State-Level Performance Indicators.* Denver, Colo.: Education Commission of the States, 1994.

Ewell, P. T., and Jones, D. P. *Assessing and Reporting Student Progress: A Response to the "New Accountability."* Denver: State Higher Education Executive Officers, 1991.

Ewell, P. T., Parker, R. W. and Jones, D. P. *Establishing a Longitudinal Student Tracking System: An Implementation Handbook.* Boulder, Colo.: National Center for Higher Education Management Systems, 1988.

Hossler, D. *Enrollment Management: An Integrated Approach.* New York: College Entrance Examination Board, 1984.

Hossler, D., Bean, J. P., and Associates. *The Strategic Management of College Enrollments.* San Francisco: Jossey-Bass, 1990.

Kemmerer, F. R., Baldridge, J. V., and Green, K. C. *Strategies for Effective Enrollment Management.* Washington, D.C.: American Association of State Colleges and Universities, 1982.

Lenning, O. T., Beal, P. E., and Sauer, K. *Retention and Attrition: Evidence for Action and Research.* Boulder, Colo.: National Center for Higher Education Management Systems, 1980.

Mallette, B. I., and Howard, R. D. (eds.). *Monitoring and Assessing Intercollegiate Athletics.* New Directions for Institutional Research, no. 74. San Francisco: Jossey-Bass, 1992.

Middaugh, M. F. "Persistence." In M. A. Whiteley, J. D. Porter, and R. H. Fenske (eds.), *The Primer for Institutional Research.* Tallahassee, Fla: Association for Institutional Research, 1992.

Pascarella, E. T., and Terenzini, P. T. *How College Affects Students: Findings and Insights from Twenty Years of Research.* San Francisco: Jossey-Bass, 1991.

Ruppert, S. S. (ed.). *Charting Higher Education Accountability: A Sourcebook on State-Level Performance Indicators.* Denver: Education Commission of the States, 1994.

Sherr, L. A., and Teeter, D. J. (eds.) *Total Quality Management in Higher Education.* New Directions for Institutional Research, no. 71. San Francisco: Jossey-Bass, 1991.

Spady, W. "Dropouts from Higher Education: An Interdisciplinary Review and Synthesis." *Interchange,* 1971, *1,* 64–85.

Terenzini, P. T. "Student Attrition and Retention." In J. A. Muffo and G. W. McLaughlin (eds.), *A Primer on Institutional Research.* Tallahassee, Fla.: Association for Institutional Research, 1987.

Tinto, V. "Dropout from Higher Education: A Theoretical Synthesis of Recent Research." *Review of Educational Research,* Winter 1975, 45 (1), 89–125.

Tinto, V. *Leaving College: Rethinking the Causes and Cures of Student Attrition.* Chicago: University of Chicago Press, 1987.

Wing, P. *Higher Education Enrollment Forecasting: A Manual for State Agencies.* Boulder, Colo.: National Center for Higher Education Management Systems, 1974.

PETER T. EWELL *is senior associate at the National Center for Higher Education Management Systems in Boulder, Colorado.*

At Arizona State University, longitudinal files have changed the way institutional researchers can look at students to answer management questions.

Arizona State University: Student Tracking in a University Setting

John D. Porter, Melinda A. Gebel

Arizona State University (ASU) is a large public research university located in one of the fastest growing metropolitan areas in the United States. As a result, many kinds of students enter ASU, including first-time, transfer, re-entry, non-traditional, commuting, and minority students. By creating longitudinal student files capable of tracking each student's curricular history from entry until graduation, our research staff can easily highlight important relationships between educational experiences and outcomes that are not apparent from other data sources. This chapter describes the structure of these files, how we create and maintain them, and how they have evolved over the years. At the same time, it provides illustrations of the many ways we have used longitudinal files to conduct different kinds of studies and to inform the institution's management.

Point-in-Time Versus Longitudinal Files

Institutional research offices at most postsecondary institutions extract frozen files in fixed-length format to answer questions about their students. These point-in-time files are the bread-and-butter data source institutional researchers use to determine how many students share a particular characteristic or may be affected by a specific policy. Examples of the kinds of questions point-in-time files can address include how many minority students enroll and how many students are on probation. Other questions require following a student over a period of time. These questions tend to focus on the proportion of a particular student cohort that exhibits a specific behavior or outcome. Examples of these questions include the graduation rate for the institution and the number of times students change majors.

NEW DIRECTIONS FOR INSTITUTIONAL RESEARCH, no. 87, Fall 1995 © Jossey-Bass Publishers

To respond to the time-based questions often asked by ASU's management, the institutional research office began building longitudinal student files in the late 1980s. The first such file was a student characteristics file designed to respond to the questions most often asked, such as student persistence and graduation rates. The second longitudinal file focused on student financial aid and includes variables on the types of financial aid our students receive over time. This file allows us to answer questions such as the impact of financial aid on student persistence and graduation, or whether certain types of financial aid contribute to academic success.

Figure 2.1 illustrates the general file design we use for the student and financial aid longitudinal files. As in many computer files, the student's Social Security number (SSN) is used as a key element for matching or extracting information. Because the longitudinal files are used for aggregate analysis, student names and other personal information are omitted. Both of these files are updated with frozen point-in-time information drawn from the university's permanent records as needed, and both are maintained as free-standing datasets associated with a particular entering cohort.

A primary goal in building longitudinal files is to merge information on entering student characteristics that remains unchanged with a set of variables that change each term. Efforts to track students over an extended period are complicated by the fact that individuals within a given cohort enroll for varying numbers of terms. For example, students entering in the fall of 1985 and tracked for ten years might enroll for a minimum of one term to a maximum of thirty terms (based on ASU's three terms per year). To accommodate this variability, ASU's student longitudinal file provides term data in a variable-length record format. The result is that variables such as course registrations, which have multiple occurrences within each term, are captured as fixed-length trailer segments to the variable-length term record. ASU's longitudinal student financial aid file has a similar structure: a set of demographic variables is included in a fixed-length header record, followed by financial aid data in a

Figure 2.1. ASU's Longitudinal File Design

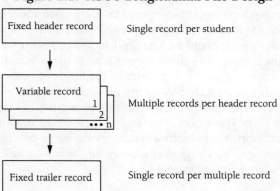

variable-length record format. These variable-length records then have trailer segments containing term and financial award data in fixed formats. The construction and use of each of these two distinct longitudinal files are described in the following sections.

ASU's Student Longitudinal File

Designed to provide complete academic histories for each enrolled student over a ten-year period (fall 1985 through fall 1995), the student longitudinal file contains extracted data from several data bases that archive information on applications, admissions, course registrations, grades, and degrees awarded. Figure 2.2 illustrates the overall design of ASU's student longitudinal file, combining both fixed-format and variable-format records.

The fixed header portion of the record stores information on student demographic characteristics at time of admission, such as high school GPA and class rank, entrance exam scores (ACT and SAT), and transfer institutions attended. Although students may attend numerous institutions before enrolling at ASU, the file accommodates data for a maximum of four transfer institutions in order to conserve space. If more than four transfer institutions exist, a variable in the term record indicating the total number of transfer hours captures any missing information for a given term. Whereas the demographic, high school, and exam variables remain unchanged with each subsequent update of the longitudinal file, the transfer data reflect the most recent information available about each student. The final component of the file is a two-digit term counter (1 to 30), which tells the researcher the number of terms that a student actually was enrolled. The total length of this portion of the file is 146 characters, containing 33 variables. Because the file is fixed in length, 76 characters are reserved for up to four possible occurrences of transfer institutions, although for some students no data may actually appear in these fields.

Figure 2.2. Student Longitudinal File Design

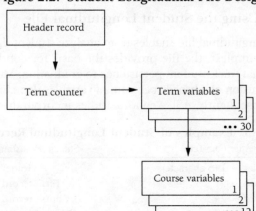

The second portion of the record consists of four sets of term-related variables: variables captured at the term census date, such as registered hours, academic level, and flags indicating the campus of registration (ASU has multiple campuses); end-of-term variables, such as term earned hours (hours actually completed by the end of the term), term GPA, cumulative earned hours, cumulative GPA, and date of withdrawal (if applicable); demographic information that might change over time, such as residency, major, zip code, and athletic eligibility status; and variables reflecting degree completion during the given term (if applicable). The total length of each term record is 91 characters and each contains 42 unique variables.

The third portion of the student longitudinal file provides information on course registrations during a given term, including course identification, department of course, course credit hours, and grade received at the end of the term. Because this section is restricted to a fixed-length format, a maximum of twelve courses per term is imposed to conserve space. A two-digit course counter indicating the number of courses for which a student registers precedes the course record. Information describing individual courses is captured in nine variables with a total length of 20 characters. Because 12 occurrences are possible, the total length reserved for the course record is 240 characters. With the two-digit course counter, the overall length is 242 characters.

The maximum length of each term record is 91 and its fixed-length course-trailer segment is 242. However, the student longitudinal file is designed to accommodate a maximum of 30 terms (three terms per year for a ten-year period). Consequently, the maximum record length for the term record and the course trailer is 9,990 characters. Adding that number to the fixed header (144 characters for the demographic variables plus 2 characters for the term counter) brings the file to a total potential record length of 10,136. Figure 2.3 illustrates the difference in the size of the record for a student attending one term versus a student attending for ten years, and shows dramatically how these files can grow.

Applications Using the Student Longitudinal File

ASU's student longitudinal file enables us to analyze student data in a number of ways. At its simplest, the file provides the basis for conducting student cohort studies that track student persistence to graduation. More importantly, it allows the inclusion of a broad spectrum of variables depicting the nature of persistence. Consequently, ASU's cohort studies incorporate additional vari-

Figure 2.3. Examples of Student Longitudinal Record Size

Nonpersister After One Term	*Student Persisting Ten Years*
Header = 146 characters	Header = 146 characters
Term record = 91	Term record = 30×91
Course record = <u>242</u>	Course record = <u>30×242</u>
Overall record length = 479	Overall record length = 10,136

ables that provide a better understanding of why students may or may not persist at the university. Such variables often include frequency and type of changes in major (changes into or out of particular majors), changes in residency status, changes in full-time/part-time status, changes in academic status (such as good standing or probation), and performance in certain courses or sequences of courses.

Another advantage of the student longitudinal file is that the file provides a mechanism for categorizing students after the fact. Most cohort analyses focus on grouping students according to entering characteristics and comparing persistence and graduation rates among the resulting groups. Studies using longitudinal files can track an entering cohort through graduation, identify characteristics that appear to contribute to persistence, regroup the original cohort based on those characteristics over time, and reanalyze the data for differential rates in persistence or graduation. For example, an initial analysis of an entering cohort may indicate that students who graduate appear to have fewer course withdrawals than those who do not graduate. Grouping the cohort on the basis of number of times courses are dropped and rerunning the analysis allows the calculation of one-year persistence rates, two-year persistence rates, and other data that can be compared among groups for differential impacts.

The student longitudinal file also allows the researcher to backtrack to obtain historical information. For instance, in a study of fall 1994 seniors who had earned more than 160 hours (typically, 126 to 140 hours are required for graduation in degree programs), the longitudinal file was used to identify a subset of students who had graduated from ASU in a prior semester, and were enrolled in a second baccalaureate degree program. The longitudinal file easily provides such information for analysis, eliminating the need to access additional data files.

A final example of ASU's use of the student longitudinal file involved examining the course-taking patterns of students. Student transcripts typically update course entries with the most recent information, including grade replacements and course repetitions. It is therefore difficult to determine the student's actual academic status before repeating a given course. By providing a term-by-term snapshot of all courses in which a student enrolls, the longitudinal file provides more accurate information about course repetitions. For example, we identified first-time students who repeat certain math courses and readily tracked each student's academic profile before and after each course repetition. Using the longitudinal file, it was easy to summarize the impact of course repetitions on student academic progress.

ASU's Longitudinal Financial Aid File

Designed to provide complete financial aid histories over a ten-year period, the longitudinal financial aid file extracts data from several data bases containing information on academic performance, economic background, and financial aid. By bringing academic and financial aid variables together in a single record, ASU is able to analyze how the allocation of financial aid relates to academic performance.

As is also the case for the student longitudinal file, building a file of this nature presents challenges. The amount of information captured makes the file unwieldy and as a result, the dataset is difficult to store and process. At ASU, the average student takes five years to graduate. During this time, the student may attend up to fifteen terms (ten terms during the academic year and five summer terms). Accommodating this amount of data in a single file requires that part of the file be fixed-format and part variable-format (see Figure 2.4).

Also like the student longitudinal file, the fixed-length portion of the financial aid file contains student characteristics that do not change or that are important to document upon entry. This header portion contains the file key (SSN), date of birth, ethnicity, SAT and ACT scores, and permanent zip code. Because ASU receives many transfer students from the Maricopa County Community College District, the fixed-length header also accommodates three occurrences of transfer institution. The final variable is the counter variable, which tells us how many occurrences of the variable-length year record follow. All together, the fixed-length header contains 116 characters.

In the variable portion of the longitudinal file, there may be one to ten occurrences of the financial aid year record. Each occurrence contains three fixed-length term segments and six possible financial aid awards. The year record contains the student's major, residency, total financial aid budget, total family contribution, adjusted gross income, and number of dependents. The reason for capturing these variables on an annual basis is that financial aid is budgeted and awarded on a yearly cycle that begins in September and ends in August of the next year. The total number of characters in the year record is 92.

Figure 2.4. Financial Aid Longitudinal File Design

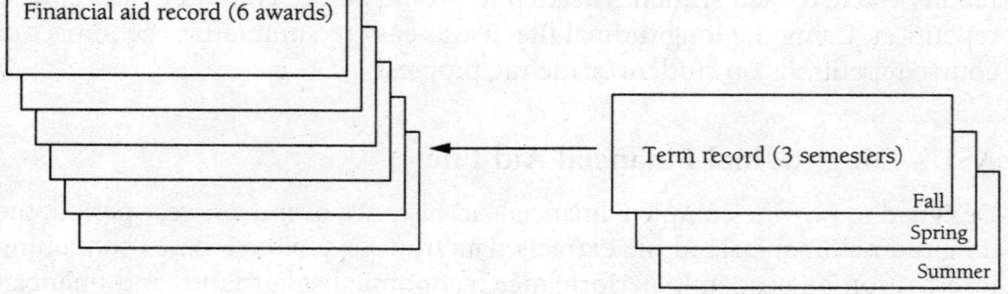

The term record contains one segment for each term during the financial aid year (in this case fall, spring, and summer terms). This part of the file contains a term identifier, term registered hours, term net earned hours, term GPA, cumulative earned hours, cumulative GPA, and a flag indicating whether the student made satisfactory progress. *Satisfactory progress* is a financial aid term that indicates whether the student meets federal requirements for completing a specified percentage of the credit hours attempted. The total length of the term segment is 75 characters (three terms of 25 characters each).

The final part of the variable-length portion of the longitudinal file is the financial aid award segment. This segment contains up to six occurrences of award data for each term: financial aid award code, fund code, award amount, and amount paid to the student. The six occurrences of award variables total 210 characters, but one of these records is attached to each academic term, so the total length is 630 characters.

The size of the ASU financial aid longitudinal file can also vary considerably, depending on whether the student attends one year or ten years. However, the average student who takes five years to graduate has a record totaling 4,101 characters. With 8,000 new students starting each fall term, it is easy to understand why this file is difficult to build, update, and manipulate.

Applications Using the Financial Aid Longitudinal File

ASU's financial aid longitudinal file offers us numerous opportunities to explore the relationships between student financial aid and other student behaviors, such as what kinds of packaging leads to better first-year retention for particular types of students, or whether accumulating student loan indebtedness has a systematic impact on student persistence or other kinds of enrollment behaviors. These relationships are largely unresearched at individual institutions. Although this shortfall is recognized in the field, the time and expertise required to create longitudinal files in the financial aid area are lacking at most institutions. For instance, one of the challenges in creating the file was adapting to the many changes in student financial aid policy that have occurred over a ten-year period. Recognizing that the institutional research office did not have the expertise to adjust for these changes, ASU included members of the financial aid office in the file design. The result was a file that both offices could use for analysis.

An early example of the use of this file involved computing the level of student indebtedness from entry until graduation. Of special concern to ASU's management was how much debt students at-risk accumulated if they failed to persist. As a result of this analysis, financial aid counselors were better able to package financial aid for at-risk students. Other applications using the financial aid longitudinal file involve investigating the relationship between financial aid packaging and student persistence. For example, by entering longitudinal data over time into a path-analytic model, we confirmed that working on campus contributes to student persistence when other factors such as academic preparation are controlled.

Perhaps the most meaningful use of the longitudinal financial aid file was an investigation into the relative fairness of financial aid packaging for various student groups based on institutional policies for allocating aid. For example, a major concern of ASU's management is that minority groups not be disadvantaged in the award process. By using data in the longitudinal file, institutional research documented the composition of the financial aid packages of various minority groups and showed how student packages changed over time.

Lessons Learned

ASU's overall experience with constructing and using longitudinal files is positive. Once such files are built and in place, they constitute a rich source of data for institutional research. However, building and working with longitudinal files presents many challenges. The following are the principal lessons we have learned in working with these files over the past six years.

Ease of Use. Given available technology, we have found that using freestanding longitudinal files to conduct various kinds of analyses is much easier and requires fewer manipulations than attempting to answer the same question by accessing multiple point-in-time files. Time and time again, ASU's purpose-built student longitudinal file has helped us to provide answers to management's ad hoc questions about student performance quickly and accurately. However, the financial aid file is used less often because of its size and specialized content. As noted in our conclusion, moreover, recent advances in technology may allow us to move to a client-server environment in which users can track students through relational data base structures without the need for a purpose-built longitudinal file (see also Chapter Five).

Flexibility. A well-designed longitudinal file allows researchers to respond to a broad range of questions. In particular, these files allow us to address questions from three different perspectives, depending on the starting point. First, the file provides a point-in-time snapshot of a given term; second, it provides the opportunity to extract historical data from prior terms; third, it allows students to be tracked progressively over time. However, the flexibility of longitudinal files extends only as far as the record layout. The physical size of these files quickly forces the institutional researcher to make value judgments about which variables to include and which to exclude. Obviously, the more variables excluded, the less able the file is to help the researcher respond to ad hoc questions.

Effort. Longitudinal files require a significant investment to build and maintain. Because data are extracted from many different sources, building and updating such files takes time. Often, we attempt to access our longitudinal files only to realize that they have not been updated for the last term! We find it difficult to allocate the staff time needed to maintain these files when there is no immediate question to answer.

Cohort Stability. Longitudinal files are structured around student cohorts, and our experience at ASU is that entering cohorts differ from year to year. Such differences can become especially important when subsets of cohorts are analyzed, as when we calculate persistence rates for individual ethnic groups. Often, such cohort variations are perplexing to management because the most recent cohort for one reason or another may go against the trend. As a result, institutional researchers need to encourage management to look at more than one cohort when examining longitudinal data in order to level out the inevitable annual fluctuations.

File Size. One of the major decisions to be made in building a longitudinal file is how many time periods to include. This decision is difficult to alter later on and should be based on an assessment of the questions that the file must address. Both of the longitudinal files we built at ASU are based on ten-year cycles. In retrospect, this time period probably was two years longer than necessary because the vast majority of students had either graduated or dropped out permanently by that point. However, each institution must make this decision based on its own experience. A good rule, however, is to discontinue tracking after more than 95 percent of the student records in the cohort have not been active for two years or more.

Conclusion

ASU's use of longitudinal files for student tracking has significantly changed the way we look at students and, as institutional researchers, the ways we go about our work. However, longitudinal files require a noticeable degree of maintenance each academic term in order to yield these benefits. The physical size of the record demands that data manipulations be performed on large computing platforms. This goes somewhat against the current direction of technology, where workstations are replacing many applications formerly run on mainframes.

In this regard, we expect client-server technology to change how ASU uses longitudinal files in the future. Three years ago, we began implementing a data warehouse concept to provide staff with increased access to various kinds of data. Warehouse data are stored in relational data bases that can be easily viewed in spreadsheet form. One of the first data bases created for the warehouse contained student data for the past ten years. Although limitations imposed by the software and the sheer size of the files involved mean that the data warehouse is not as fast as the longitudinal file in tracking students, it is much easier to use and provides greater access. The institutional research office is currently exploring ways in which longitudinal data sets can be incorporated into the data warehouse, making more sophisticated student tracking capabilities available to individual academic departments. Another technological development we are exploring for student tracking is the multidimensional data base (MDS). MDS's provide aggregate data "sliced" in ways that are meaningful to the institution or decision maker. MDS's offer ease-of-use and speed to users, but do not have the flexibility of larger relational data bases. Also, MDS's require more effort to develop and maintain than do longitudinal data files and relational data bases.

Regardless of the direction taken, today's technology is making student tracking easier and approaches like these will ultimately be more prevalent. Over the years, however, ASU's purpose-built longitudinal files have served the university well and continue to be a sound and proven approach to the increasingly important problem of tracking students that can be followed by virtually any type of institution.

John D. Porter is director of the Office of Institutional Analysis and data administrator at Arizona State University.

Melinda A. Gebel is principal planning and management analyst in the Office of Institutional Analysis, Arizona State University.

This chapter describes the development of a two-year college's ability to track students, with particular emphasis on applying this capability to evaluating developmental education.

Amarillo College: Tracking in a Two-Year College Context

Stanley I. Adelman

Amarillo College is a two-year multipurpose community college located in Texas, and was one of the founding members of the Texas Longitudinal Evaluation Student Tracking and Reporting (LONESTAR) consortium-based student tracking effort. In this chapter, I describe the evolution of student tracking activities at Amarillo College in three stages: early efforts at tracking that pre-date LONESTAR, operating LONESTAR, and more recent developments.

World Before LONESTAR

In January 1980, as a new institutional researcher, I first learned the definition of *cohort*. Amarillo College had a new Hewlett-Packard HP III minicomputer. Unfortunately, I did not speak COBOL, and the computer center staff had a backlog of programs to convert. The production of any kind of tracking data would have to wait for such pedestrian items as registration and payroll systems. Mandatory external vocational education reports to outside agencies, however, would not wait. Darrell Conger, the director of the computer center, and I agreed that if he could extract a data set, I would program the necessary report in FORTRAN. That FORTRAN program was used at the college for more than ten years. Microcomputers were not an option. Even an extract file would not fit on a 180K floppy, and that was state-of-the-art at that time.

During that first year, Darrell and I collaborated on a number of other projects. In each instance, Darrell used COBOL to extract the data I needed and I used FORTRAN to analyze it. The combination worked, but Darrell was already working overtime. Fortunately, he found a new data retrieval and report-writing tool: *Quiz*. According to the brochure, *Quiz* could produce reports directly from the data base of any HP computer. In addition, the program could extract summary data sets that could be saved and could then link those data sets together later. The company (Cognos Limited) agreed to let us try the program for thirty days without buying it. Rarely has a tool met a need so well: Darrell no longer had to prepare extract data sets and I no longer needed FORTRAN to analyze them. I could also use Quiz's extract capability to build summary files each semester that could then be linked together by Social Security number to track cohorts of students. About the same time we bought a second tool, Statistical Package for the Social Sciences (SPSS), that had just been released for the HP platform. Student tracking at Amarillo College was born.

First Attempt at Tracking. I used my first tracking files to study fall 1981 to spring 1982 retention. The variables investigated included gender, ethnicity, marital status, hours enrolled, major, birth year, basis for admission (first-time in college, transfer, continuing, re-entry), educational objective, high school, day or night attendance, hours attempted, veteran status, entering academic status, the Nelson-Denny reading test score, and the fall GPA. We expected educational objective to be a powerful predictor of attrition behavior. It was, but attempted hours was an even better one. Surprisingly, GPA was a very poor predictor, and this flew in the face of both logic and the results of published research. Surely students with higher grade-point averages would be more likely to return to the college, but this did not appear to be true. I had just encountered my first experience with a powerful intermediary variable.

I solved the mystery by treating GPA as a criterion rather than a predictor variable. Actually, I used three GPAs: the overall group GPA, the GPA for the students in the group who returned to Amarillo College, and the GPA for the students in the group who failed to return. As shown in Table 3.1, I found that at Amarillo College, GPA performance and attrition behavior are inversely proportional when students are grouped by hours attempted. The data in this case are from fall of 1993 and spring of 1994.

The reason was soon apparent. Part-time students tend to be older and less interested in earning a degree. This difference between them and full-time students masked any relationship between GPA and retention when I used GPA as a predictor. However, the GPA of those who returned remained substantially higher than that of those leaving. Patterns like this were present not only for all students, but for virtually every single-predictor subgrouping. I had already learned a lot about the ways different types of students behaved at my institution by tracking them longitudinally, but it had taken a lot of work to do it.

Table 3.1. GPA and Percentage Return by Hours Attempted

Hours Attempted	All Students		First-Time Students	
	GPA	% Return	GPA	% Return
1–3	2.86	47.5	2.62	59.2
4–6	2.66	57.2	2.42	52.9
7–11	2.53	71.0	2.09	64.5
12–up	2.64	78.0	2.44	77.7

Producing Graduation Rates. *Quiz* extract files were flexible enough for me to use them to calculate graduation rates. I limited my initial study to a cohort of first-time-in-college students entering in fall 1981. Using the *Quiz* report writer, I then linked students meeting that description in the fall 1981 extract file to subsequent spring and fall extract files, and to annual graduation extract files. I had enough room on the report for a column of major names, a column indicating the number of majors during fall 1981, eight columns to indicate the percentage who were present during each subsequent spring or fall semester, and a final column to show the graduation rate. I had a grandfather who never used one nail if more would fit; following in his footsteps, I used a tracking period of four-and-a-half years for a two-year college because that's what would fit across the page. The Student Right-to-Know Act and its 150 percent tracking period was still seven years in the future.

I actually produced two reports: one for all first-time-in-college students and one for all full-time first-time-in-college students. I included these reports in the college's databook; each year as the cohort matured, the tables contained two more columns of semester data. Finally, in the fall of 1985, I used *Quiz* to produce the final results. These showed clearly that full-time students graduated at higher rates than did part-time students. Students in technical majors graduated more often than did students in transfer majors. The latest in this series of cohort studies, printed in the fall of 1994 and using essentially the original methodology, tracked the fall 1990 entering cohort.

First Look at Developmental Education. Amarillo College had offered developmental education courses in reading for a number of years before I arrived in 1980. The director of the program and her faculty believed strongly that they had an effective program. However, many on campus believed either that the program was ineffective or that students had a "right to fail." The college policy strongly advised students assessed as reading below the ninth-grade level to enroll in developmental reading courses. Students reading between the ninth and twelfth grades could choose to enroll in reading, but were not required to do so.

When asked to conduct an evaluation, we initially developed three measures of the effectiveness of remediation (Adelman, 1982): fall-to-spring retention rates, fall course-completion rates, and cumulative grade-point averages (GPAs). We found that students who were advised to enroll in developmental reading (reading below the ninth-grade level) actually had a higher fall-to-spring retention rate than did students for whom enrollment was optional and whose assessed reading scores were higher. In fact, the poor readers returned at the same rate as did those reading at the thirteenth grade level. The ninth-through twelfth-grade readers who chose to participate in remediation had a much higher retention rate than their peers who chose not to participate. We acknowledged, however, that these results might be because of the nature of the students. Those who chose to participate in remediation could well have been more highly motivated to succeed.

Although we looked at the course-completion rates of students in their developmental classes, we were far more interested in their course-withdrawal rates in subsequent semesters. The target group here included all students who had successfully completed a reading course during the fall semester. The comparison group included all other students enrolled at the college in the subsequent spring semester. Students who successfully completed a developmental course were far less likely than other students to withdraw from courses the following semester.

Finally, we examined grade performance, although the topic proved difficult. We could easily calculate a GPA of all coursework for those who had enrolled in reading classes, but we could never find a valid group to compare them to. Second, we knew that the GPA measure did not take course-withdrawal behavior into account. Ultimately we chose two comparison statistics, though both had flaws: the semester GPA for all students and the semester GPA for those who were reading below the ninth-grade level but had not enrolled in reading. Results were as follows:

GPA for those enrolled in reading	2.24
Semester average GPA for all students	2.70
GPA for those needing but not enrolled in reading	1.79

Despite the flaws in our study, the college moved toward mandatory remediation for those reading below the ninth-grade level. It continued to allow those reading between the ninth- and twelfth-grade level to choose remediation. Once this occurred, we used the ninth- through twelfth-grade readers as a comparison group. Those reading below the ninth-grade level who were required to participate in remediation consistently outperformed the new control group on all three measures: retention, course-withdrawal rates, and GPA. By 1985, the college's Academic Affairs Committee began to require testing and (in some cases) remediation in mathematics and writing as well as in reading. Clearly our study had achieved some impact.

Some New Evaluation Techniques. As a measure of the effectiveness of developmental education, GPA dissatisfied us, but we had been unable to find a good alternative. However, a new emphasis on mathematics and writing helped to clarify the purposes of developmental education. With reading we had attempted summative evaluation because we thought that reading proficiency affected all facets of academic success. Mathematics and writing had far narrower scopes; summative evaluation in this case would more appropriately consist of performance in college algebra and first-year composition. From this we were able to derive a new criterion for success (Adelman, 1987). All three developmental areas (mathematics, reading, and writing) involved sequences of several courses. In order to enroll in a course, a student had to either test at that level or earn a grade of C or higher in the prior course. To move on to the next course, the student had to earn at least a C.

Following this logic, we decided that the most useful measure of remediation effectiveness would be performance in the next course in the sequence. Viewed from this perspective, the control group for remediation was automatic: at any level of remediation (other than the first), the target group would be those who had remediated to that level; the control group would be those who had tested into that level. It remained only to define performance. We avoided GPA for two reasons. First, the GPA measure ignored course withdrawals, which constituted about 20 percent of the actual grades in mathematics and writing. Second, students did not need a high GPA to proceed to the next course; they needed only a C or higher. Consequently, we chose as a measure of success the number of students receiving grades of A through C, divided by the total number of students enrolled in the designated course on the census date.

Using this measure, we first discovered that in both mathematics and writing, students who completed the most basic developmental course never successfully completed the subsequent course. Second, we found that those who completed the course immediately before first-year composition performed as well in first-year composition as did students who did not need remediation. Third, we found that very few students (fewer than ten) tested well enough to enter college algebra in the first place.

As a result of these findings, the English faculty revised the developmental writing curriculum. In mathematics, the faculty split the intermediate three-hour course (a combination of high school algebra I and II) into two three-hour courses. In addition, they changed basic mathematics from a one- to a two-hour course. The changes in writing showed immediate results: since the change was made remediated students invariably have performed as well as or better than students not needing remediation. The changes in mathematics also showed beneficial results. Students completing basic mathematics in the fall performed better in beginning algebra the following spring than did those who tested directly into the course. However, when we measured performance in beginning algebra during the fall term, the opposite finding was true. This sawtooth pattern, which was minimal at first, has continued over time and the swings have become larger. We found a similar pattern from beginning algebra to intermediate algebra: the remediated group has continued to be more successful when they took algebra in a following spring term, and less successful if the course was taken in a following fall term. We have made plans to further analyze this situation. Are students forgetting the math they learned over the summer, or are they enrolling in summer remedial classes that are not as rigorous as those offered during the fall and spring terms?

Tools for This Period. Throughout most of the period 1981–1986, I performed all tracking studies using *Quiz* to extract data and, in many cases, used *Quiz* to develop the necessary reports. I also used Quiz to prepare data files for analysis by SPSS on the HP computer. In 1986, however, SPSS published SPSS PC+. It cost less than the annual lease on the HP, and within three years the savings would pay for the new AT class microcomputer we purchased to run it. This change in computing platforms caused some minor changes. Data files now had to be downloaded. Fortunately, HP had a product called

AdvanceLink that has continued to be very effective, both to download files, and to serve as a terminal emulator on the HP itself. Second, because of the magnitude of SPSS output, print files had to be uploaded to the HP to take advantage of line printers. Again, *AdvanceLink* solved the problem. However, we had yet to create a true multipurpose tracking system.

Advent of LONESTAR

In December 1986, representatives from several Texas community colleges met in Austin to create a common tracking system that could be used to evaluate developmental education (Adelman, Ewell, and Grable, 1989). The group had contracted with the National Center for Higher Education Management Systems (NCHEMS) to help produce a computer program to meet their needs. At that meeting, we decided that the focus should be somewhat broader: the evaluation of developmental education would remain a focus, but the resulting tracking system should be able to support general program outcomes assessment as well. The group agreed to the following set of design goals: the tracking system would enable evaluation of developmental education, it would have to run on most mainframe computers, it would have to run on microcomputers, it would enable evaluation of all credit programs, it should incorporate a number of useful effectiveness reports, and it should be easy to set up and maintain.

Over the next six months, NCHEMS produced a system called the Longitudinal Evaluation Student Tracking and Reporting (LONESTAR), which met most of the design criteria (some of us believe LONESTAR is easy to set up and maintain; others are not so sure). NCHEMS decided to code the system in SPSS because it ran on most mainframe computers, and SPSS had just released a version for microcomputers. In June 1989, NCHEMS published a "final" data element dictionary and user's manual (Ewell, Parker, and Jones, 1988), but NCHEMS had made interim versions available to participants from the summer of 1987 forward.

Since that time, the LONESTAR users' group has included approximately forty colleges from Texas and some neighboring states (Louisiana, Oklahoma, and New Mexico). The group sponsors two meetings a year and one "bootcamp." The users' group approved significant additions to the data element list in 1992, and again in 1993, to better meet the needs of four-year universities and to take advantage of new state-level data sources about subsequent employment and transfer behavior.

How It Works. In one sense, LONESTAR is nothing more than a set of agreed-on definitions and some common reports based on those agreements. Each college maintains its own tracking files. Writing the mainframe data base extract programs to load appropriate data elements into the tracking system fields is the biggest cost of LONESTAR. The system requires two mainframe extract programs: one to define a cohort and another to provide semester performance updates.

To use LONESTAR, colleges must provide the programming necessary to write these extracts. At Amarillo College, I used *Quiz* to write the extract programs in 1987. At another institution that uses a commercial student data base package, the dean of students paid a programmer $6,000 to write the extracts during the summer of 1993.

Once a college had completed this (sometimes daunting) task, the rest was quite easy. The LONESTAR SPSS code maintains the cohorts: each semester, the researcher creates a new cohort for the term and uses the performance file from that semester to update each existing prior cohort. Using a 486DX2–66 micro, I can update a cohort in about fifteen minutes. It takes less than two minutes to update the LONESTAR program to work with a specific cohort, and it takes the computer between five and ten minutes to run the program, depending on the number of students in that cohort. Because the program runs in SPSS under Windows 3.1, I can spend this time working on other tasks (including updating the program to work with the next cohort). When the program has finished running, it automatically produces a series of mean and frequency tables on basic variables in each cohort in order to help the user verify that the program has worked correctly.

When NCHEMS delivered the June 1989 documentation, it concluded its contractual arrangements with the LONESTAR users' group. In 1992, the Texas Higher Education Coordinating Board (THECB) made available to all Texas public community and technical colleges two additional important sources of information about students who have left the college or graduated: the Federal Interagency Commission on Education code of any public Texas institution to which students have transferred, along with the CIP code of each student's major and the number of hours in which each student enrolled, drawn from the state's unit-record enrollment system; and the standard industry code (SIC) of the employer for which the students worked, along with the quarter and year, and the total wages paid during that quarter, drawn from the state's unemployment insurance wage-record data base.

Because I wanted to use this new information for program evaluation, I wrote some additional SPSS programs to enhance the LONESTAR system to take advantage of them and shared them with the users' group.

By the summer of 1993, moreover, a number of LONESTAR colleges were also experimenting with analyzing large numbers of electronic transcripts in the Electronic Transcript Network (ETN) format (see Chapter Six). A number of us agreed on the ETN-derived tracking fields that would be useful if included in LONESTAR, and proposed them to the users' group, which accepted them.

Using LONESTAR. Operating in the LONESTAR analytical environment, a number of new capabilities were available. In the realm of developmental education, LONESTAR allows me for the first time to show, by level of remediation needed, the developmental program completion-levels for all students in mathematics, reading, and writing. Table 3.2 summarizes outcomes for the fall 1990 first-time-in-college cohort as of fall 1993, by remediation need in writing.

Table 3.2.

Remediation Need	Number	Percentage Completing Regular First-Year Composition
Total group	624	59
Severe	61	16
Moderate	185	37
Unneeded	378	75

Before LONESTAR, I could track course-to-course articulation; now I can see an entire pattern of development across courses. The new reports also created lively discussions about the real purposes of developmental education and whether, based on the reports, our programs were meeting those purposes. More specifically, they stimulated a debate and ultimately a joint research project among institutional researchers at three institutions: San Jacinto College, Brazosport College, and Amarillo. What worried us particularly was the ultimate outcome of our programs: only 16 percent of those with severe needs in writing ever ended up completing first-year composition. I then added an additional factor, after arguing that the program should not be held responsible for the fact that successful students may choose not to continue. This modification showed some promise, as over 50 percent of both the severe- and moderate-need groups passed the last developmental course they had attempted.

We also considered other possible indicators of success. For example, students who complete a basic mathematics, reading, or writing course may find it easier to pass employment tests at area employers. Finally, an extended analysis was agreed on by the three institutions, which could be coded in LONESTAR. Table 3.3 presents actual output from this extended model for developmental writing.

Because all three colleges were using the same tracking system, we could debate what approach should be used to evaluate developmental education. We also needed to write the code only once in order to produce information all of us could use (Bailey, Adelman, and Preston, 1995).

Another new application arose in August 1991, when the U.S. Department of Education circulated a "Dear Colleague" letter explaining what each college must provide to prospective students under the Student Right-to-Know Act (Farrell, 1991). Again, LONESTAR provided an avenue to code a common program once for use by all member colleges. This proved particularly important because Right-to-Know has also been a moving target. When I first wrote the program, I included only the first-time-in-college students who had declared a major. Amarillo College offers both two-year associate degrees and certificates of completion of varying length. If a student had not declared a program, how could I determine 150 percent of the expected time? After I circulated the program to the users' group, we agreed that I had misinterpreted the "Dear Colleague" letter. All full-time students should be tracked and, after three years, should be examined to determine whether any have transferred to a senior

Table 3.3. Writing Performance Tracking Report for Fall 1990 First-Time College Students as of Fall 1993 Term

	Number Enrolled	Completed First Course	Attempted TASP Test	Passed TASP Test	Attempted Next Level	Passed Last Course Tried	Attempted College Writing	Completed College Writing	Earned Degree or Certificate	Transferred to a Senior College	Employed After College
Total	624	440 71%	402 64%	368 91%	116 19%	413 66%	484 78%	361 75%	71 11%	111 18%	481 77%
Entry level											
Level 2	61	38 62	21 34	16 76	23 38	31 51	13 21	10 77	3 5	4 7	42 69
Level 4	185	120 65	99 54	83 84	93 50	100 54	93 50	69 74	15 8	13 7	142 77
Level 6	378	282 75	282 75	269 95	0 0	282 75	378 100	282 75	53 14	94 25	297 79

Note: TASP is the required developmental test in Texas. Transfer is limited to Texas public senior colleges. Employment can be determined only if the student's employer participates in Texas' unemployment insurance program.

institution or have completed a degree or certificate within 150 percent of the expected time of the degree or certificate that they completed.

A final example of how LONESTAR can be used is in examining postenrollment outcomes. In Texas, the statewide Automated Student Follow-up System (ASFS) provides community colleges with transfer and employment data on their graduates and former students. It also hosts an annual statewide meeting using this information. When the sponsors asked me to make a presentation at the June 1994 meeting, I decided to merge ASFS data with a particular LONESTAR tracking subpopulation: students receiving federal financial aid. I did so because I believed a destructive stereotype exists that students receiving federal funds are really lazy people who apply for funds just to get the money and then don't fulfill their enrollment obligations.

I compared backgrounds and subsequent outcomes for all first-time-in-college students entering in fall 1990 who enrolled for six or more hours of coursework. I found first that a higher percentage of the financial aid recipients than of other students needed remedial work in reading and writing. They also tended to have parents who did not finish high school, tended to be single parents, and were more likely to be 25 years old or older. However, I found that this group was more likely than others to complete first-year composition and college math, and that they were twice as likely to graduate. SPSS produced the graphs for that presentation directly from LONESTAR files. I then linked the graphs to a Harvard Graphics presentation and used a laptop computer to display the information (Adelman and Ewell, 1995).

World After LONESTAR

Last year, Brazosport College and the Dallas Community College District secured a grant to rewrite LONESTAR in FoxPro, a microcomputer data base package. LONESTAR+ should be easier for novices to use because of powerful query-by-example routines available through FoxPro and the fact that all cohorts will now be stored in a single integrated data base. The new product should combine the tracking power of the original LONESTAR system with an easy-to-use point-and-click information system (see the Additional Resources section of this volume).

At the same time, the Community and Technical Colleges Division of THECB asked community college chief academic officers to propose a technique to evaluate the transfer functions of community colleges, using data available at the state level, in a manner similar to that described in Chapter Four. Turning to other outcomes, the Texas ASFS tracks students who leave an institution at a given time into the work force, as described in Chapter Seven. Finally, in 1993, a number of community and four-year colleges used the ETN format to send senior college transcripts to the community colleges from which the students had come. Community colleges could then determine the proportion of students transferring who were in good standing at the transfer institution (see Chapter Six).

Given these new developments, we at Amarillo have the opportunity to use tracking to evaluate our programs in much greater detail. This year, for the first time, we have included general transfer and employment performance in the program evaluation process. Ultimately, each program must determine what it expects completers to be able to accomplish, just as the developmental educators have already done. Tracking will be needed in those endeavors as well, and fortunately we will have the tools to do the job.

References

Adelman, S. I. "Another Approach to Evaluation: A Spoonful of Sugar." *Journal of Developmental & Remedial Education,* 1982, *6* (1), 25–27.

Adelman, S. I. "Evaluating Remedial Education in Higher Education." Paper presented at the Association for Institutional Research 27th Annual Forum, May 4, 1987.

Adelman, S. I., and Ewell, P. T. "Flexible Use of Longitudinal Tracking Files to Investigate Financial Aid Recipients." Paper presented at the Association for Institutional Research 35th Annual Forum, May 31, 1995.

Adelman, S. I., Ewell, P. T., and Grable, J. R. "LONESTAR: Texas's Voluntary Tracking and Developmental Education Evaluation System." In T. H. Bers (ed.), *Using Student Tracking Systems Effectively.* New Directions for Community Colleges, no. 66. San Francisco: Jossey-Bass, 1989.

Bailey, R. R., Adelman, S. I., and Preston, D. L. "The Saturday Night Special-Remediation." Paper presented at the LONESTAR User's Group Spring Meeting, April 20, 1995.

Ewell, P. T., Parker, R., and Jones, D. P. *Establishing a Longitudinal Student Tracking System.* Boulder, Colo.: National Center for Higher Education Management Systems, 1988.

Farrell, M. J. "Dear Colleague" letter. Washington, D.C.: United States Department of Education, Aug. 1991.

STANLEY I. ADELMAN is data base coordinator and director of institutional research at Amarillo College and board member of the LONESTAR Student Tracking Consortium.

The ability of states to track students from one institution to another
has markedly enhanced researchers' ability to examine complex
educational career paths for different kinds of students.

Tracking in Multi-Institutional Contexts

Alene Bycer Russell, Mark P. Chisholm

Many important issues in higher education can be best understood by examining longitudinal information about student careers. Indeed, student tracking seems to be becoming commonplace at public colleges and universities these days, and a certain level of knowledge about retention, graduation, and time-to-degree has come to be assumed by both institutional administrators and external publics. However, students' careers do not start and stop when they attend a single postsecondary institution. Many students attend more than one college over their lifetimes: they may transfer from a community college to a four-year institution, take the reverse route, move from one state to another, alternate between school and work, or follow any number of other paths. Student educational careers do not begin at the time they enter college; success in college is closely linked to elementary and secondary school experiences. Success in the workplace depends on the skills and knowledge college graduates and nongraduates bring with them to their jobs. As society asks more complicated questions about how well our educational institutions are doing, the need for better information on student careers has increased tremendously. Multi-institutional tracking capabilities can greatly enhance our ability to address these needs.

First and foremost, multi-institutional tracking requires a multi-institutional student data base—that is, student unit-record data drawn from multiple institutions located in a particular state or other geographic area. Such data bases are a relatively new phenomenon, developed in the past ten years, and are not yet found in all states. These data bases depend on the presence of substantial compatibility of data elements among the component institutional data systems and on the use of common identifiers. They also require that issues of confidentiality of student records be resolved.

The first section of this chapter describes the development of multi-institutional data bases at the state level based on a survey of higher education agencies in the fifty states conducted by the State Higher Education Executive Officers (SHEEO) in February and March 1995. These agencies, commonly called SHEEO agencies, include both state-level coordinating boards and governing boards. In a few cases, additional information was gathered from system-level governing boards. Results of this survey allow us to paint an up-to-date picture of statewide and systemwide data bases in terms of their numbers and scope of coverage. The evolution of statewide student tracking capabilities is then described, and we examine uses of these data bases, including those restricted to single-state data bases and those involving data sharing across agencies and states. Finally, the survey allows us to examine the unresolved issue of confidentiality of student records and the possible future development of this issue.

The second section of the chapter describes the construction and uses of a particular multi-institutional data base in Colorado. This system has been in place since 1986 and now contains ten years of data. Graduation and transfer rates can be computed using this data base for both within-institution and within-system analyses. The data base has proven to be of great value to the state's higher education agency and is supported by the institutions because it allows researchers to conduct systemwide analyses and because the ability to do analyses centrally reduces institutional reporting burdens.

Development and Scope of Multi-Institutional Data Bases

The development of statewide, student unit-record data bases represents an important point in an evolutionary process that began with the emergence of state higher education agencies in the 1960s and early 1970s. In the early years, these newly formed SHEEO agencies collected, synthesized, and reported data drawn from individual institutions. Typically, this included data on enrollments, revenues and expenditures, facilities, faculty, and staff. In order to produce statistics that were meaningful and consistent across institutions, these agencies worked to establish common definitions and reporting formats. Most often, they gathered only aggregate data, however, and did not have access to individual student records. This meant that tracking of students as they moved from one institution to another was impossible.

As demands for information grew, SHEEO agencies responded by developing statewide data bases. In many cases, institutional mistrust of centralized information and fear of compromising student confidentiality interfered with data base development. By the end of the 1970s, only a quarter of the states had some kind of statewide or large systemwide student data base. During the 1980s, however, growth continued at a more rapid pace, and by the end of that decade, three quarters of all states had a statewide or large systemwide student data base. Such data bases, which contain unit-record data on individual students, have now been developed in approximately forty states, affording state agencies great flexibility in conducting research. Based on the 1995 SHEEO survey, Table 4.1 summarizes the current status of statewide student data bases.

Once established, these data systems have not been static. Over time, statewide data bases have become more inclusive in terms of the number of institutions and sectors included and the frequency of data collection. New data elements have been added and new types of data bases have been assembled at the state level. Table 4.2 summarizes the types of data currently residing in statewide student data bases.

Clearly, student enrollment data are the most universal type collected. These provide states with the raw material for constructing enrollment reports and most other kinds of studies. Information on completions is needed for student tracking and analyses of the types of degrees granted. Applicant data provide states with additional information on the admissions process and institutional admissions standards. Financial aid data enable state researchers to study patterns of state and federal financial aid and to address questions of access to higher education. Student course data permit the analysis of many academic questions, including use and success of remedial courses. Assessment and performance data are quite varied, ranging from statewide basic skills test data, a gateway exam that all students must pass before they can enroll as juniors, ACT student opinion data, enrollment status, and GPA. Data on student outcomes after college typically include information drawn from alumni follow-up surveys, but is increasingly related to data-sharing with other organizations (see Chapter Seven).

Development of Statewide Student Tracking Capabilities. The full potential of statewide data bases is not realized until information from different semesters or quarters can be linked together using a common student identifier—that is, until student tracking capabilities are developed. Fueled by state interest in better understanding student retention in the mid to late 1980s and encouraged by such federal legislation as the Student Right-to-Know and Campus Security Act of 1990, the next step in this evolutionary process began to take shape in the early 1990s. Building on existing term-by-term student data bases, many states went one step further and began to track the academic progress of individual students. Statewide tracking systems of this kind have two major advantages over institutional tracking systems. First, state-level systems are more efficient; rather than every institution in a state developing its own tracking system, information can be analyzed centrally and provided back to institutions. Second, and more importantly, these systems allow tracking across institutions, providing more complete information on student outcomes: which students actually drop out, which students transfer and later graduate, and so on.

Clearly, where such state or system-level data bases exist, the demand to track students across institutions is strong. Where such data bases do not exist, the desire to track students across institutions is a primary impetus for many states to develop them. Progress in student tracking has therefore been steady. When SHEEO last surveyed state agencies on this topic in 1991, only twelve

Table 4.1. Current Status of Statewide Student Unit-Record Data Bases

Comprehensive statewide data base exists at the SHEEO level, containing student records from four-year and two-year public institutions:

Alaska	Louisiana	North Dakota
Arkansas	Maine	Ohio
California	Maryland	Oklahoma[a,b]
Colorado[a]	Massachusetts	South Carolina
Connecticut	Minnesota[a,b]	Tennesse
Georgia	Missouri	Texas
Hawaii	Nevada	Utah
Idaho	New Hampshire	Virginia[a,b]
Illinois	New Jersey	West Virginia
Indiana[a]	New Mexico	Wisconsin
Kentucky[a]	North Carolina	

Statewide data base exists at the SHEEO level, but it is not comprehensive:

Mississippi[c]	South Dakota[c]	Washington[e]
Oregon[c]	Vermont[d]	

Significant multi-institutional data bases exist, but not at the SHEEO level:

Florida[f]	New York[g]

More limited multi-institutional data bases exist:

Arizona[h]	Pennsylvania[i]

No multi-institutional data bases exist:

Alabama	Kansas	Nebraska
Delaware	Michigan	Rhode Island
Iowa	Montana	Wyoming

[a] Also contains student records from at least some independent, nonprofit colleges.

[b] Also contains student records from at least some proprietary schools.

[c] Contains four-year institutional data only.

[d] Separate data bases exist for the University of Vermont and the Vermont State Colleges System.

[e] Limited unit-record enrollment data exist, but more complete records on financial aid recipients are collected; extensive tracking capabilities exist across state agencies.

[f] Although no data base resides at the Postsecondary Education Planning Commission, separate data bases exist for the State University System, the State Board of Community Colleges, and the Florida Education and Training Placement Information Program. These data bases are linked, and students can be tracked across systems.

[g] Separate data bases exist for SUNY and CUNY.

[h] Limited multi-institutional files exist, separately for three four-year institutions and for community colleges.

[i] A data base exists for the State System of Higher Education, but is not linked to other institutions' data.

states were using a student unit-record data base to report graduation and completion rates and another twelve were in the middle of planning or developing this capability. Less than four years later, the tracking of entering first-year students is possible in thirty-five states, and the remaining five states that have multi-institutional data bases are now working on developing this capacity. Tracking transfer students—a relatively new concept—is now possible in thirty-four states, and only one state with a unit-record data base does not intend to develop this capacity. Thirty states can now track students who begin in terms other than fall, and five expect to develop this capacity.

As an aside, use of the Social Security number (SSN) as the student identifier is the clear method of choice for student tracking. In nearly every statewide data base, the SSN is used as the personal identifier, and all but one state use SSNs for student tracking. Several states not currently tracking students are trying to acquire SSNs from institutions so that student tracking will be possible.

Uses of State Data Systems. The uses of statewide student data bases are many and varied. Table 4.3 summarizes twelve common uses, in order of frequency mentioned by survey respondents. Clearly, some uses, such as Integrated Postsecondary Educational Data System (IPEDS) reporting, reflect the traditional roles and capacities of SHEEO agencies and do not require student

Table 4.2. Types of Statewide Student Data Bases

Data Base	Number of States
Enrollment	40
Degree completions	35
Applicants for admission	15
Financial aid	22
Student courses	23
Assessment/performance	15
Student outcomes after college	9

Table 4.3. Use of Statewide Student Data Bases

	Number of States
Persistence, completion, and time-to-degree studies	33
Student transfer studies	32
Studies of minority students	32
Enrollment projections	25
IPEDS reporting (fall enrollment and completions)	24
K–12 feedback reports	23
Remedial education studies	22
"Report card"/accountability reporting	21
Student Right-to-Know Reporting (intended use)	20
Financial aid studies	18
Studies of admissions standards	17
Vocational-technical reporting	11

tracking systems. However, the three most common uses of statewide student data bases—persistence, completion, and time-to-degree studies, student transfer studies, and studies of minority students—illustrate the added value of multi-institutional student tracking capabilities. Without the ability to track students across institutions centrally and efficiently, it is virtually impossible to imagine how comparable information might be generated.

Student tracking from the first year through college departure addresses only part of the picture of student postsecondary careers. Many statewide data systems are now beginning to address other important policy issues such as what happened before the student entered college and what happens after he or she leaves. One new and rapidly growing phenomenon is the development of linkages between state higher education data bases and those maintained by other state, federal, and private agencies and organizations (see Chapter Seven). Table 4.4 summarizes the states currently engaged in this type of activity. Combining data-sharing arrangements already in place with those exploring such possibilities, data sharing with the K–12 sector and with state employment agencies appears to be most common.

Unresolved Issue and Future Prospects. One of the recurring issues in student tracking across agencies is confidentiality of student records. Currently, agencies respond in a variety of ways to confidentiality issues. Many states are attempting to follow guidelines from the Family Educational Rights and Privacy Act and some have put additional state policies in place. For example, some states provide records with SSNs attached only when confidentiality is guaranteed and these identifiers are necessary for a particular analysis. In other cases, states have established predefined lists of possible users. Additional states provide unit-record data, but scramble the student identifier so that individual students cannot be identified. Some states do not have clear or written policies, but review requests for data sharing on a case-by-case basis. Some use a data-sharing agreement form. Still other states are beginning to experiment with informed consent procedures in which they request student permission in advance to share data with other agencies. For a final group of states, con-

Table 4.4. Interagency Data Sharing

Type of Agency	Data Sharing Arrangements in Place (Number of States)	Data Sharing Arrangements in the Discussion/Planning Stage (Number of States)
State department of education (K–12)	10	10
Postsecondary agencies in other states	3	6
State employment records	11	9
State corrections	3	3
Federal training and employment records	3	4
Military	5	2
Private sector employers	2	3

fidentiality is not an issue: they simply will not share data. As interagency data-sharing arrangements multiply, these issues will need additional resolution.

Despite these concerns, most states are very interested in expanding tracking across new boundaries. An impressive thirty-three states indicated that they are interested in developing new data-sharing arrangements with postsecondary agencies in other states, and four others replied with a more cautious *maybe*. These responses are motivated by the need to acquire greater understanding of interstate student migration patterns—to know more about what happens to high school students who leave the state, to better estimate graduation rates, and to track the employment and postgraduate education of their college graduates. Again, much caution is expressed with respect to confidentiality when using student records for these purposes.

In sum, concerns about confidentiality of student data have not disappeared, but there seems to be a greater comfort level—and even a modest enthusiasm—to embrace more open data systems. Safeguards must be put in place, of course, but institutions and state agencies are finding ways of dealing with these concerns. Indeed, significant progress has been made, but as even more extensive data-sharing arrangements arise, it is evident that more routinization and standardization of these matters are needed.

Institutional Benefits from Statewide Tracking. Technological changes have been tremendous in recent decades and have acted powerfully to stimulate data-system development at the state level. Indeed, the increasing benefits afforded by improved technology have gradually reduced institutional resistance to multi-institutional data bases, further encouraging their development. Changes in recent years include shifts from large, mainframe computers to personal computers and local-area networks, lowering costs and increasing access; faster PCs with greater memory capacities; relational data bases replacing flat-file structures, simplifying the analysis of complex questions; the development of client-server and decision-support software that puts more powerful tools into more hands; the shift from physical forms of data transfer (tapes and diskettes) to electronic forms (use of the Internet), increasing the speed and lowering the cost of data transfer, and increasing access to such electronic enhancements in electronic communication as Gopher and the worldwide web. Every day, states are moving closer to a vision in which many kinds of information—student unit record data, aggregate data, tables, reports, and national data sets—are readily accessible to a wide group of users.

These advances, reflected in evolving statewide data systems, are bringing very concrete benefits to institutions as well as statewide agencies. Where institutions previously spent countless hours and dollars producing numerous duplicative reports, statewide data systems now can produce much of the needed information directly. Thus, the reporting burden on institutions is greatly reduced. At the same time, more data are made available to institutions, particularly comparative data from other institutions and state averages. Institutions are no longer alone in searching for external peer data. Finally, for the first time, important policy questions related to student movement across institutions, sectors, organizations, and even states can be addressed. Statewide data bases are in this way providing information to institutions about later placement and performance that cannot be generated at the institutional level. State agencies can also provide the informational tools (such as decision-support software) necessary to assist institutional decision making. In sum, institutional capacity to respond quickly to many kinds of information needs and requests has been greatly enhanced.

Longitudinal Tracking in Colorado

This section briefly describes the development of a unit-record data system in Colorado and its use in longitudinal tracking. The Colorado Commission on Higher Education (CCHE) began collecting unit-record data in 1986 in response to a major legislative initiative on higher education in Colorado. The result of the legislative review was to strengthen the powers of the CCHE. These new powers included setting statewide admission standards, establishing powers of program review and discontinuance, preparing higher education budget recommendations, and conducting systemwide planning.

Before 1986, the data collection role of CCHE was greatly constrained. Backlash from an attempt in the mid 1970s to collect and report program cost data for all public institutions had led to a temporary suspension of all data collection by CCHE, and the agency's role in this area was only beginning to build back up again. The collection of HEGIS (now IPEDS) data from institutions was coordinated, and several special-purpose surveys about student enrollment were collected from institutions annually. For the preceding two years, institutions had been given the option of submitting the enrollment data on tape in a unit-record format, but the submitted data did not contain SSNs or any other student identifier. These files could be aggregated to create data tables that would otherwise have been submitted in hard copy form, but were of little use for anything else. Six of the twenty-eight public institutions continued to send the forms.

With the new CCHE role, however, institutional representatives began to argue that it was important for the agency to have the best data possible, especially if the commission were to establish and monitor statewide admission standards. In addition, the National Center for Educational Statistics (NCES) had just announced that HEGIS was to be replaced with IPEDS, and all institutions were facing substantial reprogramming of their data systems in order to respond to the revised Fall Enrollment and Degrees Conferred surveys.

A CCHE proposal to institute a Student Unit-Record Data System (SURDS), therefore, was met with broad support. SURDS was designed to produce the new IPEDS enrollment and completions data so that reporting could be done on a statewide basis and institutions would no longer need to complete these surveys; replace all existing hard-copy data collections of student and completion data; update an existing financial aid reporting system that was hard to maintain and expensive to update, but was required by state financial aid policies; and provide the commission with accurate enrollment, completions, admissions, and financial aid data that could be relied on to support commission policy development.

From the very first, CCHE staff designed the system so that institutions would be able to obtain copies of the data to enable them to conduct statewide studies of such topics as transfer patterns.

A committee of institutional and governing board representatives met with CCHE staff for almost a year to develop definitions, file layouts, and a statement of uses of the data that conformed with state and federal privacy laws. The ultimate system resulted in four files, with slightly different universes of reporting institutions (Table 4.5).

Implementation. SURDS was implemented in less than a year, by one programmer working part-time on the project. The choice of programming languages was limited to those available on the IBM mainframe available for use. Thus, the edit programs are written in COBOL and most mainframe analysis is done using SPSS. The majority of analysis, however, is done on PCs from aggregate files downloaded into Paradox and maintained on the commission's local-area network. Data are downloaded only after all files are signed-off on by the institutions as being accurate, and all published reports using the data

Table 4.5. Colorado Student Unit-Record Data System

File	Contents	Universe
Enrollment	End of term enrollment data, including demographic data enrollment status, credit hours, GPA, and degree program. Originally just collected for fall term, but expanded to all terms in 1989.	All twenty-eight public institutions and two privates starting in 1990.
Completions	All certificates and degrees awarded in the previous fiscal year (July through June), including for each degree awarded: demographic data and program. Collected at the end of each fiscal year.	All twenty-eight public institutions and two privates starting in 1990.
Undergraduate applicants	Data on all undergraduate applicants (first-year students and transfers) for each term, including demographic data, high school rank and GPA , standardized test results (ACT or SAT), GED if taken, and previous college and college credit hours and college GPA if a transfer student.	All twelve public institutions with incoming first-year students.
Financial aid applicants	Data on all applicants for state financial aid in previous fiscal year, including demographic data, family income and budget data, and type and amount of state, federal, or institutional loans, grants, or work-study received.	All public, private, and nonprofit institutions eligible for state aid (about fifty-eight total).

come from the Paradox files on the network. Only one master copy of each aggregate is maintained, ensuring data integrity and consistency of reporting over time. Data were initially submitted by the institutions via nine-track tapes, but for the last two years have been provided almost exclusively via file transfers over the Internet. CCHE is currently exploring the possibility of moving SURDS onto a client-server system.

Longitudinal Tracking. After five years of SURDS data collection, CCHE became interested in tracking students over time. The data to do this were available: SSNs for a majority of students, and enrollment and completions data for five years. However, the existing file formats and available programming languages made tracking very difficult. As part of the work from a Ford Foundation grant awarded through SHEEO, CCHE developed Cohort Tracking System (CTS)—a relational set of linked files built from the SURDS data but designed to facilitate the longitudinal tracking of students. In brief, CTS allows a selected group of students (a cohort) to be specified and then builds an extract record that shows all available data for each student in this group for the succeeding (forward tracking) or preceding (backward tracking) seven years.

CTS extracts have been used extensively by CCHE over the past several years for longitudinal tracking. Some of the particular applications have included calculating graduation rates that conform to initial student right-to-know (SRK) procedures, analyzing systemwide graduation and transfer patterns, and computing transfer rates for community colleges.

In addition, several one-time studies have been conducted that were possible only because of the availability of data of this kind. These included matching graduates with state unemployment insurance files to study the job outcomes of graduates (see Chapter Seven), conducting an outcomes study of transfers from community colleges to baccalaureate-granting campuses to evaluate their success compared to "native" students, and projecting enrollments based on historical patterns of enrollment from individual counties to particular institutions, by age and high school graduation status.

These data are also used to monitor statewide compliance with the CCHE Admission Standards Policy, to evaluate program demand for new program proposals, to review existing programs during studies of possible discontinuance, to produce legislative reports on financial aid expenditures, to provide IPEDS data on fall enrollment and degrees conferred for all public and two private Colorado institutions, and to respond to numerous ad hoc requests.

Systemwide Graduation and Transfer Patterns. A natural use of CTS was to calculate graduation and transfer rates for the public colleges and universities in Colorado. Some Colorado colleges had their own internal systems in place, but the vast majority of institutions had not invested the time and resources necessary to compute graduation rates. In addition, no institutions had data that would allow them to calculate meaningful transfer rates within the Colorado public system. Some attempts at providing registration reports from one school to another had occurred, but no consistent or complete system was in place.

The commission's report, therefore, was of great use to many institutions. New legislation in 1986 required assessment reports from each institution, and graduation rates for all institutions and transfer rates for community colleges were required as part of each institution's report. The commission data were used by many institutions to satisfy those requirements.

The first report also generated much discussion about time to graduation in the state. The statewide graduation rate for a baccalaureate after four years was about 20 percent. In other words, only one out of five students who first enrolled as full-time, degree-seeking students in the state had completed a baccalaureate degree after four years. The range of completion rates across institutions varied from about 40 percent to less than 5 percent. This range of variation was not significantly different from national comparative data for similar types of institutions, but the low percentage was still shocking to many, especially those who thought of a four-year institution as producing degrees that would take four years to complete. Partly as a result, several bills have been proposed in the Colorado legislature over the past several years that deal directly with graduation rates. Specifically, these bills direct institutions to provide more ways to guarantee that a student who wants to graduate within four years is able to do so.

Because only four years of data were available, the initial graduation-rate report computed rates for only four years. Subsequent reports now track graduation for six years for the fall 1986, 1987, and 1988 classes. One of the problems with this type of analysis is that computing graduation rates is a little like looking at a distant star. One is looking backward in time. To compute a graduation rate after six years, one has to wait almost seven years from initial enrollment before the necessary data are available, and the delay is often difficult to explain to busy policy makers.

Student Right-to-Know. When the first Notice of Proposed Rule Making for the SRK legislation was introduced, the commission's CTS data base was able to respond. Seven years had elapsed since SURDS was first adopted, and a six-year graduation rate could be computed for all Colorado institutions. Given great confusion in the institutional research community about the SRK rules, the ability of the commission to compute the required rates was greatly appreciated by all the colleges. The commission staff produced a report for each institution that followed, as closely as possible, a sample form distributed by the NCES. The institutions were then free to either submit the form to comply with the reporting required in June 1992, or to submit alternate data that they had generated themselves. This particular report has not been produced subsequently because the federal reporting requirement is currently in abeyance, and the format of the report was not of particular use to the institutions. Similar reports that better match Colorado policy needs, however, are generated on an annual basis.

Commission staff have also used the data capabilities of CTS to evaluate subsequent proposals by the Department of Education about SRK rules and regulations. Many of the proposed rules would have created a system to which CTS could not respond or that would have been very difficult to implement. This analysis has been used in preparing responses about the impact of proposed rules and regulations, and in making suggestions to the U.S. Department of Education about how such rules and regulations might be formulated.

Transfer Rates for Community Colleges. Arthur Cohen, at the University of California at Los Angeles, has been conducting a study for several years on transfer rates from community colleges to four-year institutions (Cohen and Brawer, 1987, 1989). A transfer, for the purpose of these studies, is a student who enrolls for the first time at a community college, completes at least twelve credit hours at that college, and then enrolls at a four-year institution within four years. The transfer rate is the percentage computed by dividing all transfer students by the total number who enroll for the first time and complete twelve or more hours. CTS has been used to report this rate by racial/ethnic group for all fifteen community colleges in Colorado for the 1986 through 1989 classes. The data system permitted Colorado to participate in the study and to assemble comparison data from several hundred community colleges at no additional cost to the institutions. The actual report was generated from the data maintained on the commission's Paradox data bases, and was completed in less than a day.

Conclusions. The CTS and SURDS are invaluable to the Colorado Commission. The data are used to support many of the policy needs of the commission; in particular, the ability to do longitudinal tracking has been of benefit to the institutions (especially community colleges attempting to evaluate the effectiveness of their transfer programs) and has influenced policy discussion at both the state and national levels.

In Colorado, as elsewhere, the critical issues of our times will continue to demand better information about students and how they progress through school and through the workplace. As traditional patterns of college attendance further give way to nontraditional patterns, student tracking questions become even more complex, demanding new linkages across postsecondary institutions and other parts of society. In the past two decades, tremendous progress has been made in many states to establish the capacity for multi-institutional tracking. The benefits of this progress are only beginning to be realized, and we can expect them to increase in the future as the need for answers to ever more complicated questions arises.

References

Cohen, A. M., and Brawer, F. B. *The Collegiate Function of Community Colleges: Fostering Higher Learning Through Curriculum and Student Transfer.* San Francisco: Jossey-Bass, 1987.
Cohen, A. M., and Brawer, F. B. *The American Community College* (2nd ed.). San Francisco: Jossey-Bass, 1989.

ALENE BYCER RUSSELL *is research associate at the State Higher Education Executive Officers in Denver, Colorado.*

MARK P. CHISHOLM *is director of institutional research at the University of New Mexico.*

*This chapter examines several developing technologies and
recommends strategies for reengineering student tracking systems.*

Harnessing New Technologies
for Student Tracking

Victor M. H. Borden

In recent years, many articles relating to higher education research and administration start out by sounding the alarm on increased demands for public accountability. Interest in student tracking systems predates this most recent outcry but has been accentuated by both external pressures and institutional management needs. More importantly, these same sources of interest have started to reshape the task of student tracking. On one hand, political, economic, and social trends have changed the questions and issues faced by researchers and decision makers. On the other hand, emerging information technologies have changed the methods and expectations for deploying student tracking systems.

This chapter briefly examines the changing context of demands for student tracking systems and discusses in detail several emerging technologies that provide the tools to respond to these challenges. After reviewing the role of technology in various stages of student tracking system development, discussion focuses on how these emerging technologies may affect the activities, roles, and responsibilities of those who are charged with developing student tracking reports and analyses.

Changing Context for Student Tracking

In Chapter One, Peter Ewell described many changing political, social, and economic conditions that have influenced higher education accountability requirements generally and student tracking efforts specifically. The changing demographics of the national college student body represent these changing conditions and the challenge in responding to them. By 1990, nearly one-half

(47 percent) of all undergraduate students were age twenty or older and over 30 percent were age twenty-five or older (EDSearch, 1994). The changing demographics belie more important changes in students' economic circumstances, preparation, needs, and course-taking habits.

Before considering the ways in which developing technologies can be used to reengineer student tracking systems, it is important to note how they have and will continue to change the context for student tracking. Perhaps more than any other aspect of societal change, emerging technologies hold the greatest potential for reshaping the experience of higher education. The changes technology affords may help to best address the needs of the growing numbers of nontraditional college students.

In a recent address to the Association for Institutional Research, Twigg (1995) described a possible scenario in which 20 million new full-time-equivalent students will be generated by U.S. workforce requirements of the early twenty-first century. According to Twigg, these students' higher education needs will challenge our current higher education institutions beyond the ways in which nontraditional students have so far. Twigg describes the necessary transition as one from faculty-centered curricula with professionally provided student support services to student-centered curricula with just-in-time learning. That is, the tradition of classroom lecturing to students who attend school full-time while living at college will increasingly give way to multimedia-based contact across computer networks to students at home, at work, and at other technology access points.

Green and Gilbert (1995) note the limited impact of new technologies on the academic practices to date but suggest that significant change is both inevitable and desirable. They point to the increased number of nontraditional students who already benefit from new distance education applications of technology. They also describe stages of development by which new technologies may further affect the course and content of teaching and learning. As these changes occur, Green and Gilbert argue that we may not be able to compare the new and old ways of doing business because the basic objectives and methods of delivering a college-level education will change significantly.

Plater (1995) proposes that emerging technologies and changing student demographics demand a transformation toward individualized student curricula that remove the time- and place-bound limitations of most current higher education institutions. Plater argues that the basis of student assessment will shift from time-on-task to competency and performance mastery. Moffet (1994) takes these ideas even further, suggesting that today's educational institutions will be replaced by distributed learning networks characterized by self-directed and self-assessed learning.

It is difficult if not impossible to predict precisely how emerging technologies and changing individual and societal needs will affect higher education in the coming years. It is clear, though, that the notion of college as a four-year experience for the eighteen- to twenty-two-year-old well-prepared learner is a myth that has outlived its usefulness. Student tracking analyses must also break away from this outdated paradigm and facilitate the transformation of higher education assessment. Toward this end, we must rethink the concepts and methods of student tracking from systems design through dissemination. The remainder of this chapter explores the ways in which developing technologies can be used to facilitate the reengineering process.

New Technologies for Student Tracking: A Guided Tour Through the Information Systems Production Cycle

Although technological trends have influenced the need for reengineering student tracking systems, they can also play a large part in forming the solution. In effect, these technologies provide new platforms for diving into deeper, muddier waters that they have helped create. The desktop computers in widespread use today offer more power, speed, and memory than the mainframe computers of ten years ago. It is now possible to process millions of student records on a standalone desktop computer.

An increasing number of desktop computers no longer stand alone. Many are connected to local- and wide-area networks that, in turn, connect to other computers within a college or university and around the world. These connections allow the user to communicate with others and to harvest data from a wide range of data bases from within and outside the institution. The management of data resources has become a task independent of the applications from which these data were created. At the front end of today's computers are a growing number of graphically oriented natural-language end-user tools that help one to navigate through networks and data bases without having to master cryptic programming languages.

It seems that the pace of technological advancement is faster than our ability to incorporate new tools into daily work routines. Part of our ability to adjust to these changes is to understand more generally the direction in which these changes are moving. In the next section, we view these changing tides by taking a tour through the systems design process.

Stage 1: Problem Definition and Systems Specification

The demand for student tracking analyses and systems derives from both internal and external information needs. Like other institutional analyses and information systems, student tracking efforts must be guided first and foremost by the stated needs of the information consumer. Also, as with many other analyses and systems, the needs of the consumer are often not well-articulated and may contain seemingly contradictory objectives. The uncertain and changing context within which the developer works makes it necessary for him or her to stay abreast of institutional, regional, and national developments. That is, student tracking systems developers must learn from what others have said and done before them.

Information technologies can greatly facilitate this learning process. Yesterday's trip to the library can now be supplemented, if not altogether replaced, with searches through worldwide networked resources from a computer attached to the Internet. It is currently possible to connect to hundreds of library collections through the Internet. On-line services, such as the CARL UnCover, allow the user to locate relevant articles and have them faxed to one's office or home. (CARL UnCover is a comprehensive index to periodicals developed by the Colorado Alliance of Research Libraries; URL telnet:\\database.carl.org.) AskEric (URL http://eryx.syr.edu) is an example of a searchable data base containing references more specific to studies on topics of interest to higher education researchers.

The U.S. Department of Education's Gopher Server (URL gopher://gopher.ed.gov) contains reports, tables, downloadable software, and even primary data sets from the National Center for Educational Statistics collections. A rapidly expanding number of national and state agencies, as well as institutions, professional associations, interest groups, and even individuals are adding relevant materials to Internet sites each day. The researcher is further aided by available search engines that allow one to identify potentially relevant resources on this quickly changing platform. (A list of web-based search engines is available through URL http://home.mcom/home/internet-search.html.)

The Internet also provides opportunities for exchanging information among professionals. Electronic newsletters, special-interest listserv lists, USENETs, and public bulletin boards allow the interested researcher to identify and communicate with colleagues working on similar topics. The Association for Institutional Research electronic newsletter routinely posts requests from people attempting to locate resources for a local study of interest. (Back issues of the AIR electronic newsletter, which include subscription information, are available from the URL http://ike.engr.washington.edu/general/air.html.)

The number of gopher, web, and ftp servers on the Internet is growing at a phenomenal rate. The Internet is quickly becoming the first point of access for finding research and professional resources related to any topic of inquiry. It is also evident that the Internet can play a central role in other phases of systems development.

Stage 2: Data Extraction and Synthesis

The next step in building a student tracking system is to identify appropriate sources of data and extract the data into the analysis and reporting environment. When conducting tracking at an institutional level, one typically depends on the institution's student record system for much of the data. However, these data are rarely in a form directly amenable to tracking studies.

The traditional solution for bringing student tracking data together is to create a longitudinal data base from coordinated point-in-time extracts. Because one cannot readily recreate the past, it is necessary to have the foresight to routinely and systematically capture point-in-time data. Many institutions do so as part of state and federal reporting requirements, but the data needs for student tracking often go beyond the data required for external accountability purposes.

There are several notable limitations to longitudinal student tracking data bases. For one, traditional tracking systems best accommodate traditional cohorts—that is, following a cohort of first-year, full-time students through college. Given the increasing interest in student retention at various levels of higher education and the increasingly transient nature of college student populations, tracking becomes far more complicated than just following a traditional cohort.

The ability to define and track student cohorts should be more flexible and adaptive than traditional tracking data bases have allowed. Tracking systems should be able to accommodate diverse and changeable cohorts and link data from a variety of sources, including student record data, institutional surveys, and external data resources.

Linking an institution's student data with data from other educational institutions or from state employment agencies provides an opportunity to track students beyond a single institutional experience and obtain significant follow-up outcomes. Chapters Six and Seven provide further information on the importance and use of these sources of data.

Taken together, the need for more flexible tracking systems and the availability of external follow-up tracking data shifts the focus of tracking systems away from a single data base and toward the capabilities to link together data from a variety of organized and documented sources. Relational data base technology provides many of the linking capabilities. Long-standing data base packages such as Microsoft FoxPro, Borland's Paradox and dBase, and Microrim's rBase have become more graphically oriented and somewhat easier to use. Newer products, such as Microsoft Access and Lotus Approach have moved away from command language interfaces toward more complete graphical interfaces.

Point-in-time extracts of institutional data themselves can provide a more flexible data resource without going through the extra step of creating a longitudinal student data base. However, they must be designed to accommodate the needs of student tracking research. For example, if one would like to define a cohort as the students who enter a certain major field of study in a given semester, then it is necessary to maintain data on either point of entry into a major, or prior semester major status. In other words, although longitudinal student records are not necessary to track students, point-in-time extracts should be longitudinally postured to minimize the data navigation requirements for tracking analyses.

Moving from longitudinal to point-in-time data structures shifts a significant portion of tracking system development from one-time data base design issues to recurrent data navigation issues. Generally, two classes of logical algorithms are required to synthesize point-in-time data into longitudinal form. One set of algorithms is needed to define cohorts and another set is needed to track the cohort over subsequent time periods (and possibly across multiple institutions and beyond college). In effect, one creates the longitudinal dataset at the time of analysis based on the needs of the specific analysis. As a result, one has additional power to redefine cohorts and tracking events to meet more specific tracking needs. On the other hand, one must be sure to have the appropriate point-in-time data to accommodate a variety of analyses.

For example, consider the cohort of students entering a specific academic field of study in a given semester. The algorithm that defines the cohort must identify students currently enrolled in the major who were not enrolled in that major during their last semester of attendance. In defining this cohort, one must consider such issues as how to accommodate students who are returning to a major after participating in a temporary program, as well as students who have taken various amounts of time off. Similarly, the follow-up algorithms must accommodate subsequent experiences such as subsequent changes of major and participation in off-campus programs that take the student away from the institution for a period of time.

Tracking algorithms can become very complex, especially as one considers nontraditional tracking analyses. The algorithms follow directly from one's desired tracking measures and represent the bridge between data synthesis and the next stage of tracking systems development: data analysis. As researchers become better able to link data from a variety of sources, the need to maintain data in a single system becomes less important. What becomes more important is the systematic capture of student information across a broader spectrum of systems.

Within an institution, the data from admissions, registration, and student billing systems must be thought of as part of a more integrated whole. Among institutions, one must consider the degree to which data definitions and process time frames allow for the tracking of students beyond a single institution's boundaries. The Standardization of Postsecondary Education Electronic Data Exchange/Exchange of Permanent Records Electronically for Students and Schools system described in Chapter Six is an example of a developing set of standards for exchanging data among institutions.

In recent years, the concept of a data warehouse has emerged for the development of wide-ranging, flexible, interconnected, and accessible information systems. The data warehouse incorporates elements of data capture, access, analysis, and dissemination. Inmon and Kelley (1994) describe the data warehouse as an integrated and standardized collection of the type of data needed in an organization to make long-term decisions. Whereas operational application systems tend to the day-to-day processes of an organization, the data warehouse focuses on the needs of tactical and strategic decision processes.

The data warehouse is an extension of the point-in-time extract concept institutional researchers have long used. In the first volume of this series, Balderston (1974) stated that "data in operating files often need to be brought together and reorganized, as the boundaries of the individual areas of operating responsibility . . . do not usually conform with the boundaries of management and planning problems" (pp. 57–58). Saunders (1977) discussed the need for institutional research practitioners to maintain lines of communication with operational offices that foster an understanding of the meaning of the data as well as the procedures and time-lines involved in data capture. Although Tetlow (1990) suggested that institutional research offices may need to develop their own data bases for analysis and planning, Borden and Delaney (1989) recognized the role an institutional research office can play in the creation of a central repository of timely, consistent, and reliable management information that would more directly serve the growing numbers of academic and administrative managers who want direct access to management information.

The data warehouse concept represents the maturation of these ideas into an information resource that includes the intelligence of a variety of information managers. It combines aspects of relational data base performance, networking and connectivity, data standardization and documentation, and measurement and conceptual modeling toward the formulation of an accessible and useable information resource for decision makers. Furthermore, a growing range of software tools are available for developing, maintaining, and deploying data warehouses. These products include multiplatform relational data base systems, data access software that allows one to incorporate business rules, and executive information system software that enables the information provider to create navigable presentations that include tabular, textual, and graphic information.

Stage 3: Data Analysis

The traditional tools for tracking analyses have been statistical software packages such as SAS and SPSS. These software packages are now available across a variety of computer platforms, including the most popular desktop operating environments. The availability of these tools on desktop computers has put more control in the hands of the analyst. It is no longer necessary to place programs in the batch queue of a large mainframe computer and compete with operational transaction systems for computer time. In addition, the graphical user interfaces of these packages make them easier to learn and use.

Spreadsheet software, such as Lotus 1-2-3, Microsoft Excel, and QuattroPro have also expanded their functionality in several ways to better serve analysis and reporting of student tracking data. Traditionally, these packages were saved for the latter stages of analysis to create tables for reporting results. However, spreadsheet software packages have greatly increased their range of data base manipulation, statistical analysis, and graphing functions, which can be used at earlier stages of tracking systems development.

A variety of other tools can be used to analyze student tracking data. The relational data base tools mentioned earlier include programming languages that allow the user to analyze and summarize data in almost any way. Almost all computer programming languages, such as Basic and C, have similar capabilities. Specialized statistical packages allow the analyst to apply specific models that are relevant to student tracking, such as those that support time-series analysis and logistical regression.

The availability of a wide spectrum of both general and model-specific tools is a source of both power and confusion. Fortunately, the tasks of data storage, data access, and data manipulation are becoming increasingly independent. Most analysis software can read data stored in a variety of formats. Furthermore, these packages can prepare output in forms that can be read by a variety of other packages. This allows the analyst to use tools with which she or he is already familiar, as long as these tools have been updated to take advantage of the more powerful operating systems and integrated data environments.

Stage 4: Dissemination

The usual way to disseminate student tracking information is to write and distribute reports that summarize the analysis, providing both quantitative information as well as explanatory and interpretive comments. One limitation to this method is that the information is delivered according to the provider's schedule, which is not necessarily coordinated with the needs of the consumer.

Emerging technologies can be used to improve information dissemination in two general ways. First, the report writer can use tools that enable him or her to bring information together more quickly, arrange it in ways that facilitate understanding, and distribute it to prospective readers electronically. Second, the reader can access information when needed, navigate through it electronically, and even build customized versions of more general reports.

Report Writing. Word processing, spreadsheet, and graphic software are the primary tools of report preparation. Advances in each of these technologies have made it easier to prepare tables, text, and graphics. More importantly, these tools are far more integrated than ever before. It is now a simple task to place a spreadsheet table or graph into a word processing document. In fact, in the latest versions of the more integrated software suites, it is hard for the user to tell which program he or she is using while assembling a document.

There have been several important advances in spreadsheet software that can help the report preparation process. One advance is the ability to link spreadsheet templates with a variety of relational data bases. This allows the user to update tables and graphs as soon as new data become available. The leading spreadsheet products have also developed "intelligent dialogs" that lead the user step-by-step through data base queries and graph creation processes.

Other developing features of several spreadsheet software packages are pivoting and drill-down capabilities. Using these technologies, it is possible to swap quickly the rows and columns of a table and create a variable that can be used to generate tables for individual units via an embedded pop-down menu. These features may hold the greatest promise for allowing a broad base of people to create customized views from general templates designed by the research analyst.

Distributing Reports. Once assembled, student tracking information can be disseminated using many of the same technologies described in the earlier stages. Reports can be distributed via e-mail or posted on a gopher or world-wide web server. Notable limitations that have limited the use of these platforms are quickly disappearing. For example, the limitations to integrating text and graphics through gopher servers have been circumvented through desktop mail systems, worldwide web servers, and multiplatform web viewers. Furthermore, the often-cited lack of security for web-based documents will soon be addressed with security arrangements that are strict enough to permit credit card transactions over the Internet.

Web publishing systems may represent the next wave of integrated platforms for delivering navigable information resources over the Internet. These systems allow one to provide access to relational data base systems through analyst-designed forms and templates that enable the information consumer to request information for subpopulations of interest. This platform can be used to deliver high-quality customized reports directly to the consumer.

Although the Internet is the most widely supported platform for distributing information, it is not the only one. Within more self-contained units and organizations, the researcher can use local-area networks and desktop-based software to create more tightly controlled information dissemination systems. Most high-level software platforms, such as the integrated software packages of Microsoft, Novell, and Lotus, include tools that allow nonprogrammers to develop workplace applications. Spreadsheet macro languages have now been supplanted by dialog managers, object-linking and embedding, script managers, object-oriented visual programming languages, and other tools that allow one to automate processes of report production, distribution, and access.

Implications

In many ways, new technologies provide the institutional researcher with powerful tools for developing useful student tracking systems to serve a broader array of consumers. Networking and connectivity provide access to better information in the development stage as well as more timely, effective, and meaningful distribution of information. Relational data bases and data warehousing support products can allow greater access to more timely, standardized, and navigable information.

The increasing array of tools and information resources may lead to a shift of responsibility for application programming from the data processing professional to the information service provider. As a result, the person with the content knowledge could deliver his or her expertise directly to the consumer without having to go through a technical mediator.

With increasing power comes increasing expectations. As more people experience the power and range of the Internet, they will expect more from their local information support services. In some ways, these technological advances remove a set of traditional excuses for not being able to bring the right information to bear at the right time for the right people. In other ways, these changes have replaced old problems with new, higher-level problems. Table 5.1 summarizes these changes, comparing the traditional steps and results of student tracking systems with what may be in store for those who travel down these new paths.

Table 5.1. Trends in Tracking Systems Development

	What's Out	What's In
Data resources	Longitudinal student tracking files	Minimum: longitudinally postured census snapshots Preferred: data warehouse
Analysis	Flat file analysis—SPSS or SAS at every stage	Relational data base navigation—table generator; SPSS/SAS analysis; spreadsheet tables and charts, network dissemination
Tracking capabilities	Tracking the first-year cohort	Tracking variously defined cohorts into and through programs; backtracking from terminal events (graduation, withdrawal); tracking before and beyond college
Results	Frustration over the limited capabilities of traditional student tracking systems	Frustration over the endless choices in the data resource design, model development, and dissemination processes

The increasing power of information technologies allows one to consider more flexible and complex student tracking models. Variably defined cohorts, tracking beyond a single institution, and customized reports allow the researcher to accommodate a broader range of decision-making and evaluation needs. The likely result is well summarized in an anonymous quote distributed across various Listserv lists and USENETs in September 1994: "In some ways, I feel we are confused as ever, but I believe we are confused on a higher level, and about more important things."

References

Balderston, F. E. "The Design and Uses of Information Systems." In H. R. Bowen (ed.), *Evaluating Institutions for Accountability*. New Directions for Institutional Research, no. 1. San Francisco: Jossey-Bass, 1974.

Borden, V.M.H., and Delaney, E. L. "Information Support for Group Decision Making." In P. T. Ewell (ed.), *Enhancing Information Use in Decision Making*. New Directions for Institutional Research, no. 64. San Francisco: Jossey-Bass, 1989.

EDSearch. *Education Statistics on Disk*. Washington, D.C. U.S. Department of Education, Office of Educational Research and Improvement, National Center for Educational Statistics, May 1994.

Green, K. C., and Gilbert, S. W. "Content, Communications, Productivity, and the Role of Information Technology in Higher Education." *Change*, 1995, 27 (2), 8–18.

Inmon, W. H., and Kelley, C. "The 12 Rules of Data Warehouse for a Client/Server World." *Management Review*, May 1994, pp. 6–9.

Moffet, J. *The Universal Schoolhouse: Spiritual Awakening Through Education*. San Francisco: Jossey-Bass, 1994.

Plater, W. M. "Faculty Time in the 21st Century." *Change*, May/June 1995, 27 (3), 22–33.

Saunders, L. E. "Dealing with Information Systems: The Institutional Researchers Problems and Prospects." AIR Professional File, no. 2. Tallahassee, Fla.: Association for Institutional Research, 1977.

Tetlow, W. "Selecting Appropriate Computing Tools." In J. B. Presley (ed.), *Organizing Effective Institutional Research Offices*. New Directions for Institutional Research, no. 66. San Francisco: Jossey-Bass, 1990.

Twigg, C. A. *The Need for a National Learning Infrastructure*. Address delivered at the thirty-fifth annual forum of the Association for Institutional Research, Boston, May 28, 1995.

VICTOR M. H. BORDEN *is director of information management and institutional research and assistant professor of psychology at Indiana University–Purdue University, Indianapolis.*

Electronic transcripts constitute a rich source of data and, if used effectively, can add substantially to an institution's evaluation toolbox.

Tracking Students Who Transfer: Electronic Transcript Exchange

Michael J. Green

Data drawn from admissions and registration records are sufficient to support basic tracking studies, but without tools to analyze transcript files, institutional researchers lack the ability to support meaningful research about student outcomes or performance. Demand is growing for such information, both within an institution and after transfer. More and more, researchers are being asked to assess how well students perform at other institutions. This requires access to individual transcript information from these other institutions, as well as a way to analyze such data. In the past, the best any researcher could do to address this question was to review individual paper records supplied by other institutions, and either report the perceived outcomes anecdotally or laboriously hand-enter data into a tracking record.

This chapter focuses on the growing opportunities institutional researchers now have to rectify this condition through the development of standardized statewide electronic transcript formats and the national Standardization of Postsecondary Education Electronic Data Exchange/Exchange of Permanent Records Electronically for Students and Schools (SPEEDE/ExPRESS) standard. The relative ease-of-use of these formats for information exchange will be compared, and the information they contain related to student tracking noted. The underlying technical requirements needed to use this type of information effectively will also be discussed. Finally, an example of electronic transcript-sharing in the state of Texas will be examined in detail to show how electronic data exchange has been used for student tracking. The final section of the chapter discusses some future implications for researchers.

NEW DIRECTIONS FOR INSTITUTIONAL RESEARCH, no. 87, Fall 1995 © Jossey-Bass Publishers

Need for Electronic Data Interchange

Institutional researchers have several potential uses for the kind of information contained in transcripts from other institutions. The most obvious use of this type of information is simply tracking student transfer activity. Electronic data interchange (EDI) records at the very least allow researchers to determine automatically the transfer status of individual students. In the absence of accessible statewide unit-record information (see Chapter Four), such information is invaluable. However, the ability to use transcript data for this purpose also depends on the existence of a communications system for sharing transcripts among institutions. The need for consortial agreements is therefore imperative (Trainer, in press). EDI records allow researchers to assess not only whether transfer occurs but also how the institution's former students perform at the transfer institution. This later performance is of interest in itself, but becomes even more valuable when direct comparisons with the course-taking activity of the same students at the original institution can be made.

A third activity valuable to both secondary and postsecondary institutions is monitoring the effectiveness of articulation agreements with other institutions. Such agreements are the lifeblood of high schools and community colleges that are engaged directly in preparing students for other settings, but they are of interest to all types of institutions. If the programs and courses institutions offer do not directly relate to the subsequent success of students at a transfer institution, the sending institutions are not fulfilling their primary objectives. With the proper tools for analysis and monitoring in hand, articulation agreements can be updated and evaluated on a regular basis.

For these reasons, it is imperative that all institutions develop data-sharing agreements with their feeder and transfer institutions. However, setting up consortial agreements for electronic transcript sharing can be difficult and time-consuming, and institutions should not wait for the full availability of EDI capabilities to begin to establish them. Even if information can be shared initially only through the physical exchange of diskettes, the initiation of such agreements should be started as soon as possible.

Students, as consumers, also demand timely information about where they stand academically and their future potential to transfer or graduate. Partly as a result, electronic transcript information is becoming a major tool for determining student progress, both within institutions and at transfer institutions. The growing operational use of information drawn from electronic data transfer by registrars and admissions offices provides institutional researchers with an opportunity to influence the processing and use of this type of information. These offices must have timely access to transcripts in order to inform admissions decisions. Here the researcher can help representatives of these offices understand how electronic admission and registration of students can help them operationally.

At the evaluative level, electronic transcript data can provide a wealth of tracking information to the institutional researcher. However, this breadth of information is available only when a consistent and practical process for collecting and sharing such data has been developed. Here the utility of electronic transcript data depends on two major factors: the existence of consistent data definitions across all institutions participating in an exchange and a clear definition of who is a transfer student. Another stumbling block is the lack of adequate tools to aggregate or analyze the very large volumes of data involved. Effectively processing the large mass of raw data typically obtained through EDI requires software that can support comparisons of the outcomes of specific courses with one another and can allow the evaluation of overall groups of courses against their counterparts at other institutions. Software of this kind was developed through the Texas data exchange project described later in this chapter.

Types of Electronic Data Interchange Formats

Electronic transcript network (ETN) technologies promise to provide individual institutions with the ability to efficiently exchange information about student performance for purposes of comparison and outcomes evaluation. A number of statewide networks provide institutions with access to electronic transcript information. Several years ago, the Alliance for Higher Education (AHE)—a consortium of four-year institutions in north Texas formed in the early 1980s—developed a network for transferring electronic records. This system is based on a common format, copyrighted by AHE, that is used to transmit transcript files over the network among member institutions. Several community colleges joined the network in the late 1980s, which allowed them to share transcript information with transfer institutions. Shortcomings of this system were the high level of technical knowledge needed at each institution, annual fees associated with participation, and the limitation of being able to share transcript information only with other member institutions.

Although transcripts could be provided via diskette, the proprietary AHE file format limited the ability to share information with nonmember institutions. This resulted in fairly limited acceptance of the AHE format as a universal standard for transcript exchange among institutions in Texas. Less-than-universal acceptance in turn limited the availability of transcript information shared among institutions. Nevertheless, the AHE network was important in piloting the development of the kinds of formal transcript-sharing agreements and data analysis strategies needed to use EDI technology for student tracking.

A more universal format for data-sharing has recently been developed by the U.S. Department of Education in conjunction with the American Association of Collegiate Registrars and Admissions Officers (AACRAO) under the name SPEEDE/ExPRESS. This set of standard formats represents a superset of a number of previously developed state and regional electronic transcript formats, including the AHE format. SPEEDE/ExPRESS formats are accepted nationally and can be sent over any electronic communications network system. Because the formats used ensure data security, they can be transmitted over public-access networks such as the Internet. This ready availability promises to provide universal acceptance of and access to ETN technology to all schools and universities (see the Additional Resources section of this volume).

A comprehensive summary of the SPEEDE/ExPRESS standards and their accompanying data-element definitions was published by AACRAO (1993). In this monograph, full technical specifications of the system are provided, together with a description of how the SPEEDE formats were developed and how they should be used. Four standard formats (called transaction sets for electronic data interchange) have been developed for SPEEDE. They include a transcript record, a transcript acknowledgment, a request for transcript, and a response for transcript request. A complete source guide is also available that provides information about every data segment and data element in the SPEEDE/ExPRESS format (American Association of Collegiate Registrars and Admissions Officers, 1993). Other formats are also being developed and tested, including standardized applications for admissions and financial aid transcripts. The development of such additional data sets suggests that the availability of electronic data interchange will greatly influence institutional research practice in the near future, especially in the realm of student tracking.

Texas EDI Project: A Link to Student Tracking

Information on the performance of transfer students is vital for evaluating the effectiveness of any program that prepares students for further education. Most information of this type received from transfer institutions in the past was deficient in at least three ways: it was not timely, it was on paper, and it did not include sufficient detail to inform decisions about the effects of an institution's programs on the subsequent success of students at a transfer institution.

The first comprehensive project intended to assemble and use detailed performance information about transfer students using EDI technology was conducted in 1992 by a group of community colleges in Texas. This project capitalized on a prior initiative—The Higher Education Project for the Exchange of Transcripts (THEPET)—that had been completed the previous year. Experience with THEPET had determined that the Texas ETN file format described previously was a viable research tool for investigating transfer performance. The 1992 project was intended to explore two operational issues with respect to transcript sharing. The first was ease of access to information from the transfer institutions. Here the project attempted to facilitate and simplify the process of data-sharing through the use of a common electronic data format. The second issue addressed by the project was the need to efficiently manipulate and analyze the large volumes of transcript data that result from these exchanges. The project's central activity, however, was the development of a compiled program written in C++, designed to extract relevant information from received ETN transcript data and compare it with local transcript data. The output of the program allows researchers to conduct specific course-to-course or subject-to-subject comparisons of performance for transfer students before and after transfer.

History of THEPET. THEPET began as an outgrowth of the Texas Automated Student Follow-up System (ASFS). In 1989, a group of Texas community colleges initiated a system of tracking based on centralized matching of student Social Security numbers (SSNs) with the statewide higher education unit-record data base housed at the Texas Higher Education Coordinating Board and statewide unemployment insurance wage records held by the Texas Employment Commission. Using these data bases, the ASFS identified whether a given student was employed during a specified quarter and whether the student had transferred to another Texas public institution. Although these data matches represented a major advance in the ability of participating colleges to track former students, they did not provide much information about academic performance at either the original institution or at the transfer institution. The purpose of THEPET was to test the feasibility of using more sophisticated data analysis software in conjunction with electronic transcript data assembled from selected four-year institutions. Transcript data on selected students were supplied on diskettes using the proprietary format owned by AHE. This format constituted a subset of the then-emerging national SPEEDE/ExPRESS format, which has since become standard.

Procedures. The THEPET study population consisted of all students who attended a participating two-year institution and who met three additional conditions: they had completed at least twelve nonremedial or developmental credit-hours at the participating institution, they had enrolled in higher education for the first time at the participating institution, and they had attended the participating institution during at least one fall, spring, or summer term between September 1989 and December 1992. The SSN of each student meeting those conditions was used as the key for matching selected students with corresponding electronic transcript information obtained from four-year institutions. The first step in the process involved compiling a file containing the SSNs of the selected students by participating two-year colleges. These files were then sent to the four-year institutions, where the SSNs were matched against their own transcript files. One problem that arose at this point was the identification of an appropriate contact person at each university. Once the process of data-sharing becomes a normal function, the file can be received by the four-year institution as a regular part of business, and the matching can be done in a timely manner. But if the process is perceived by the four-year institution as an ad hoc research effort, it may not get the attention it deserves.

When the process functions properly, four-year institutions send a transcript corresponding to each matched SSN, in the common ETN format, back to the requesting two-year institution. At this point, the two-year institution can use the THEPET software to process the data into meaningful information for tracking and analysis.

Variable Definitions. Two primary dependent variables were used in the THEPET pilot study: persistence to the end of the term and academic performance.

Persistence to the end of the term was defined in terms of a course-completion ratio calculated by dividing the actual number of credit hours completed at the transfer institution by the total number of credit hours attempted. In general, any course in which the student earned a grade of A through F was counted as a completed course. Credit hours were determined by the awarding institution and were used without question in this study. Academic performance was measured by using the grade-point averages earned at the two-year and four-year institutions. The institutions generating the transcripts also calculated the grade-point averages, and these were used directly in the study. The approach used to assess effectiveness consisted of comparisons of performance in particular two-year courses with performance in later four-year courses with corresponding content, or for which the two-year courses were prerequisites. Comparisons for this purpose were made between English courses at both types of institutions and between mathematics courses at the two-year college and engineering courses at the four-year college.

Research Questions. The research hypotheses investigated in this pilot were as follows: that there were no differences in the persistence rates of two-year college students who transfer to four-year colleges and their persistence rates after transfer, that there were no differences in the performance of two-year college students after transfer, and that there were no differences in the specific matched course performances of two-year college students before and after transfer. Independent variables used were type of major at the two-year college (academic, vocational, or undecided), student objective at first enrollment, standard academic standing, student type (transient or not), remediation status, and ethnicity.

Processing ETN Data with THEPET Software. Four-year transcripts were processed by each participating two-year institution to generate a list of SSNs from which a set of corresponding two-year transcripts was generated. This produced two matched lists of records in two different files, one containing four-year transcripts and one containing two-year transcripts. These two files became the source files for the THEPET software, which was used to conduct the transcript analysis. This software contains two primary processing programs, both written in ANSI C. These programs access the two-year and four-year transcript files to generate two new output files in a format that can be read by SPSS. Another THEPET program, written in SPSS, matches and merges the two transcript files. This single merged file can then be used to generate standard THEPET reports pulled off a menu and written in SPSS. These standard reports present comparative statistics on such overall outcomes as the course completion rates and academic performances of former two-year college students at the four-year institution. The researcher can also use this file to conduct ad hoc analyses using SPSS (for example, to analyze particular subpopulations).

THEPET also allows the researcher to build two additional files that contain specific two and four-year course records. These files can then be used to compare student performances in related departments or to compare the outcomes of courses at the two-year institution with their counterparts at the four-year institution. For example, a researcher might investigate such issues as whether a mathematics student from a two-year institution does as well in subsequent mathematics courses at the transfer institution as he or she did in the two-year mathematics courses taken previously.

Findings. Findings of the pilot are interesting in themselves and raise a number of points associated with using ETN data for research purposes. As noted, the THEPET software allows researchers to compare grades earned in groups of courses in order to evaluate the general preparation or performance of students and allows specific course-level assessment. Results showed that, given the limitations of grades as indicators of performance, students tended to do as well at the four-year institution as they had done in similar courses taken at the two-year institution. Standard crosstabulations generated by SPSS produce a breakdown of students with less than a C and greater than a C in the selected course or subject area. These tables and a subsequent chi-square analysis showed no significant differences when results from all participating schools were aggregated. Some differences were noted, however, when students from specific two-year colleges were linked to corresponding performances at specific four-year institutions. These differences were generally attributable to unique admissions criteria, small cell populations in some of the program areas, or the specifics of articulation agreements between certain institutions.

The real implication of the pilot, however, was to prove the concept. Information drawn from ETN records is practical and can be an important component of the tracking and performance portfolio that a two-year institution has at its disposal.

What Will Researchers Be Required to Do in the Future?

The growing need to assemble student tracking files that include postenrollment performance suggests that all institutional researchers should seek access to ETN data files of the type described in this chapter. The ability to send and receive transcript files should become a priority for all institutions. Major issues associated with this priority are the difficulty of acquiring such data in the first place and the potential uses and misuses of the resulting information.

Regarding the first issue, all institutions that wish to use ETN data in student tracking must first be a member of an established transcript-exchange system or must have the capacity to convert their transcripts to SPEEDE/ExPRESS format. To actually accomplish the exchange, participating campuses must be wired as part of a regional network or have access to the Internet. Both preconditions are relatively simple to state, but may take an inordinately long time to complete. Persistence and initiative on the part of both institutional researchers and technical support personnel are necessary to establish these preconditions; in most cases, the process should also involve the registrar. A second challenge is to get priority for the required data extraction and con-version of data to the standard format from the institution's computing services department. Here it may be important for institutional researchers to work with other offices at the institution that want to use electronic transcript capa-bilities—such as admissions and registration—to ensure that developing such capability becomes a priority.

These internal problems are only the first of many topics that need attention. A next step is to obtain written agreements from the institutions from which tran-scripts are desired. These institutions must also be able to send the information by means of a network or on diskette in the format required by the receiving institution. Given this requirement, convergence of all institutions on a standard format, most likely SPEEDE/ExPRESS, is a major precondition for success. Until a majority of transfer and feeder institutions are using the same format, ETN exchange remains a research project, not an established tracking process.

Absent a standard format, research studies using ETN data must of neces-sity remain ad hoc and incomplete. Until appropriate clearinghouses to admin-ister transcript requests institutions are established, each university must respond to each requesting community college individually. This is tedious and time-consuming work. The obvious solution is to pool community college files within a given state or region, match them against available four-year institu-tional files, then have the corresponding four-year institutions create transcripts for each of the matched students identified. Community colleges could then submit batch requests against the merged file of transcripts, based on the SSNs of their students. Coordination between the relevant state higher education agencies and the state's two-year and four-year institutions is a necessary con-dition for establishing such a system. Ideally, both public and private institu-tions would be included in such a process, as is already being attempted by some states in their unit-record data systems (see Chapter Four).

A second issue associated with the use of ETN transcript data is the com-monly expressed interest of department chairs and faculty in obtaining the raw data. It is important to resist this temptation. From a research standpoint, it is unwise to allow individual departments access to such data because in the absence of statistical training, they will often try to draw conclusions about the effectiveness of their curricula based on the grade-point averages of only a few selected students. The strength of analyses that compare two-year and four-year performances lies in their ability to uncover large-scale trends or anom-alies. For example, too much emphasis should never be placed on the absolute values of any obtained differences in grade-point averages between two- and four-year institutions using these procedures. Instead, it is relative differences (among departments, types of students, or other factors) and the issues that any such differences may bring out at face-to-face meetings between commu-nity college representatives and their four-year counterparts, that constitute the real power of such data.

Analysis of ETN data is only one tool in the institutional researcher's arse-nal of analysis. Used with care, however, this tool can stimulate far more productive discussions about articulation and subsequent performance than have occurred so far. Institutional researchers should become more familiar with this kind of data as it becomes available, and should ensure that the formats used and the mechanisms established for interinstitutional exchange are designed with this end in mind.

References

American Association of Collegiate Registrars and Admissions Officers. *SPEEDE/ExPRESS: An Electronic System for Exchanging Student Records.* Washington, D.C.: American Association of Collegiate Registrars and Admissions Officers, Council of Chief State School Officers, 1993.

Trainer, J. *Participating in Institutional Data Exchanges.* New Directions for Institutional Research. San Francisco: Jossey-Bass, in press.

MICHAEL J. GREEN *is associate vice chancellor for research and planning at North Harris Montgomery Community College District, Houston.*

Researchers can use unemployment insurance wage and related files to describe and compare students' workplace status before, during, and after enrollment.

Linkages to the World of Employment

Loretta J. Seppanen

Since 1988, state governments have been collecting information on a quarterly basis from employers about employment and earnings for 60–97 percent of the workers in each state. With the exception of New York, each state's department of labor or employment security (ES) collects and maintains this unemployment insurance (UI) wage file. Its intent is to document whether an individual is potentially eligible to receive unemployment insurance benefits and set the level of those benefits should the worker become unemployed. Consequently, the UI wage file contains data for each employed worker in the state, identified by Social Security number (SSN), on such matters as total earnings, employment status, and industry of employment. Given these contents, the UI wage file also has considerable potential value for researchers in determining the labor force status of students and former students. The purpose of this chapter is to explore this potential by reviewing data-linking techniques between such administrative records and existing student data bases as a cost-effective method for obtaining information on students' work status.

Administrative records such as the UI wage file are by definition constructed and updated for routine management purposes. As a result, the collecting agency, as a part of its normal function, bears the considerable expense of data collection. Educational researchers tapping into these data bases trade off control over the timing, coverage, and type of data available in return for the benefit of obtaining fairly comprehensive low-cost data. A growing number of institutions and state systems find this a worthwhile trade-off.

States collect UI wage records under federal guidelines, but these allow states some choice regarding the specific data elements collected. As a result, there are some differences in the contents of these files across states. In New York, for instance, the Department of Taxation and Finance provides individual payroll tax records to ES for UI wage-reporting purposes. The resulting data

NEW DIRECTIONS FOR INSTITUTIONAL RESEARCH, no. 87, Fall 1995 © Jossey-Bass Publishers

are somewhat different from the UI wage data described here. Furthermore, available administrative records are not limited to wage files. Florida, which has the nation's most comprehensive data-linking system, matches data drawn from postsecondary institutional enrollment records with military enlistment records from the U.S. Department of Defense, postal career service data from the U.S. Postal Service, employment records for federal career employees from the Federal Office of Personnel Management, inmate records contained in the state's Department of Corrections data base, and records covering participation in the major welfare payment programs available from the State Public Assistance Agency (Pfeiffer, 1995). Several states also establish links with UI benefits history files, which record an individual's receipt of unemployment insurance benefits. Researchers in Ohio and Wisconsin have also used the revenue files associated with state payroll taxes as a data source. However, such files are not as comprehensive as UI wage records and not all states collect payroll taxes.

Purposes of Administrative Data-Linking

Most states that have engaged in administrative data-linking to determine labor force status have done so for two reasons: research and accountability. Although they are related, each purpose raises a distinct set of issues.

Research. In Washington, the State Board for Community and Technical Colleges (WSBCTC) first considered links with administrative records in 1989. For our student outcomes research we needed a data base that could efficiently allow us to describe student employment status during and after enrollment. At that time, we explored the possibility of combining our own management information files and other administrative records such as the UI wage file with survey follow-up data. The pilot-test results met our needs, and the addition of these administrative files to our data array provided us with a rich pool of descriptive information. The combination of administrative records and surveys continues to yield outcomes data to examine specially funded work force training efforts, to evaluate vocational education programs, and to construct several institutional effectiveness indicators. For example, the UI-wage file link allows us to regularly monitor the employment gap between graduates of color and whites and between those with and without disabilities.

The same file-linking process is also able to support the work of other researchers. The University of Maryland, for example, used the UI match to determine the economic value of university education to the state (Stevens, 1994). A Washington State University (WSU) researcher is using UI data to compare returns on investment for community college transfers versus those who begin their education at WSU. The state of Florida uses such data to study the rate-of-return by educational sector and to look at recidivism rates following prison-based education. The WSBCTC UI-linked files will soon be used for a study of the net impact of two-year college training for dislocated workers.

Accountability. At least twenty states now link higher education enrollment data with available UI wage files; leaders in the field include Colorado,

Florida, Illinois, Oregon, Maryland, North Carolina, North Dakota, South Carolina, Texas, and Washington. But in most states, accountability, not research, was the catalyst for getting started. In fact, file linking began in the mid 1970s related to accountability reporting for the Cooperative Education and Training Act federal job training program. Many two-year college systems use such methods to replace traditional vocational education follow-up surveys. As with a survey, the basic assumption is that the student's employment status after college is a useful indicator of the quality of education received. The data-linking process is simply a cost-effective way to determine subsequent employment.

Linking Process

Those who link to administrative records follow similar procedures whether they accomplish the match for research or accountability purposes. Links are generally performed by a general contractor in each state that negotiates between the data producers and the data users. In the case of UI wage records, the data producer is usually the state Department of Labor or ES, whereas state higher education boards, colleges, and universities are key data users. As the name suggests, the general contractor is in essence retained by both producers and users to accomplish the actual data link. A number of different issues determine whether the linking process is effective.

Role of a General Contractor. Some general contractors serve other users, including secondary schools, welfare offices, agencies administering the federal Job Training Partnership Act, proprietary schools, and prisons. In most cases, state law specifies who can be hired as a general contractor. The state's Occupational Information Coordinating Committee, for example, may be funded by the state to serve as the general contractor for linking purposes. In Florida, the legislature created a new entity, the Florida Education and Training Placement Information Program (FETPIP) to handle this general contractor role. The researcher can also serve as his or her own general contractor— handling all the negotiations and payments related to the link. In Washington, for instance, the WSBCTC serves as its own general contractor. It subcontracts some of the linking process to the state employment security agency and uses its own resources to link to postsecondary files.

Under a typical general contract arrangement, the institutional researcher typically has access only to summary-level findings. This is because the general contractor's agreements with data producers usually preclude sharing unit-record files that might identify individual employers. Because we serve as our own general contractor in Washington, WSBCTC has access to the unit-record file that results from the link. Summary-level data would not have met our needs because it would not have allowed us to examine patterns of employment by industry linked to the degree programs students completed.

Politics of the Process. Regardless of who acts as general contractor, the linking process is inherently political. First, it requires negotiations among organizations that have substantially different cultures. None of the data providers are funded to provide data to institutional researchers. They are in business for some other purpose. As a result, they usually need to be paid for access to their data. Even when they are paid, they may not have the staff to provide a timely record link. Based on a decade of experience, Florida's Jay Pfeiffer outlines five useful steps for working through the politics of a data-linking process: determine interest and receptivity on the part of the data provider, determine the specific conditions under which administrative records can be linked, review wage record and student record structure, context, and content, involve the agency responsible for administering the UI program, and determine who does what (Pfeiffer, 1995).

Alternatives to the Mainframe Link. A UI wage file typically resides on a mainframe computer whose operating environment is not user-friendly. In many states, employer characteristics data (such as size of firm, location, and industry type) are located in another, equally difficult-to-access mainframe computer system. Establishing data links with these mainframe files involves problems typically associated with using any legacy data system originally established for large-scale record-keeping: the need for considerable expertise in using the file and long turnaround times. Some state ES departments or third-party matchmakers have created more accessible separate research files using data extracted from base record files. The University of Baltimore is a pioneer in the use of standalone workstation storage and processing of the UI wage and employer files for educational linking. The Illinois Department of Employment Security has linked data from a number of different employment-related files. Their research data base can be linked to college records to provide eight prior quarters of wage and employment information. These standalone workstation and specially linked research files offer a considerable advantage over linking directly to the legacy systems used to manage the unemployment insurance process.

Using Other Administrative Records. As noted, Florida's FETPIP engages in data linking far beyond available UI wage records, tapping a wide range of national and state data bases. In addition to UI wage linkages, North Carolina and Washington link student records to the UI benefit history files that contain records of people who have received UI benefits over a particular time period. In using such records, it is important to remember that the UI benefit history file is limited to those who actually receive unemployment benefits, not everyone who is unemployed. However, data from this file can be combined with other available information to establish a ratio between the official unemployment rate and the number of unemployed workers who are receiving benefits to derive an estimate of the proportion actually unemployed. North Carolina also links former students with administrative records drawn from the state job-placement system, a service that is widely used by job seekers. The job-seeker file, combined with the UI wage and benefit files, provides a good estimate of the total labor force in North Carolina (Brown, 1994). However, not all states have such a comprehensive job-seeker listing.

Some of these sources produce more information than others. In Washington, for instance, less than 1 percent of former vocational students are found in the military file. Although some students who leave postsecondary institutions do end up on welfare or in prison, this fact is generally not discovered through follow-up surveys. Welfare files are therefore especially useful to monitor flows on and off of welfare, although caution is needed in interpreting results. When I first used this link, for example, I claimed that training led to a decline in welfare participation. Later I learned that nearly the same rate of leaving the welfare rolls applied to people who had not attended college. I should have done a net impact analysis before making any claims.

Linking with Other States. Graduates in a given state might be employed in other states, especially if the institution has a national reputation or is located on a state border. Unfortunately, UI wage files are state-specific and no data are contained in one state's files about employment in another. To obtain such data, general contractors must negotiate individually or via consortia with neighboring states. A lot of work is currently taking place regarding interstate matches, however. For instance, Maryland's Department of Economic and Employment Development is the lead agency in a multistate consortium that is promoting the benefits of voluntary state cooperation related to record linking. The U.S. Bureau of Labor Statistics is also designing a national data base that would support routine interstate data exchanges. The bureau is working with the agencies that keep the federal civilian and military personnel records to determine whether and how to include those records in all links to administrative records of the type described here (Stevens, 1995).

Benefits of Using Administrative Records

A number of benefits have led states to increased use of administrative data-links for student tracking. Certainly the primary one is the low cost of such procedures when compared to surveys, together with the high validity and reliability of the resulting data. FETPIP, for instance, accomplishes its comprehensive data linking for only $.07 per student. When the real cost of survey work is considered, we have found in Washington that equally valid and reliable results can cost up to $50 per respondent. The major costs of data-links are the fixed costs associated with initial programming and of management and analytical staff time. Cost for computer runs are trivial in comparison. Consequently, the cost of linking 100,000 records is only marginally greater than running a link with 25,000 records. Given these minimal additional costs, states try to link all students who leave college, not just vocational graduates. As a result, the same dollars spent on record linking provide a far more comprehensive picture of the outcomes for all students leaving the institution than is possible via a graduate survey.

Although an important noncoverage issue is associated with using administrative records, data-linking has the additional benefit of eliminating survey nonresponse bias. Survey nonresponse problems are particularly problematic for small subpopulations. Despite our efforts, WSBCTC has had difficulty in obtaining reliable survey results for Native American, Hispanic, and African-American students. Linking to administrative records, however, yields a substantial number of records for each of these groups, and thus allow us to make subpopulation comparisons.

Finally, administrative records allow researchers to examine directly the complex dynamics of employment. We know, for example, that prior work experience affects the likelihood of getting a good job (National Center on the Educational Quality of the Workforce, 1995). Administrative files allow examination of the actual extent of work experience for each student and the differential impact of that experience on employment outcomes. Similarly, there is no need to hold to a linear view of the relationship between work and education when using administrative records. Many students participate simultaneously in more than one type of training program and are employed as well. The administrative link can capture this kind of simultaneous participation, whereas only the most complex (and expensive) longitudinal surveys could provide a similar systemic perspective.

Issues in Using Administrative Records

Despite their many benefits, a number of important issues are associated with using administrative records. The most prominent for potential users are issues of timing, those associated with the actual coverage of such data files, and the confidentiality of records.

Timing Issues. The UI wage file consists of a quarterly census of employment and earnings. The state ES department allows employers three months to report after the end of each quarter. Most employers meet this three-month reporting deadline, but some report later. This means that information on the employment status of former students in the January–March period becomes available for linking in July. This first link may then be followed by links for the same time period with other states and with other higher education data bases. Most of these matches are run against large mainframe data base systems and require expert programmers and weekend processing. Systems such as those used by the University of Baltimore eliminate this delay. In Washington, where we link directly to mainframe data systems, we typically see the results of these matches in November, eighteen months after spring graduates left their colleges.

Eliminating the link with other states would save about two months, as would matching against research files rather than the original mainframe data system. Even using these short-cuts, the snapshot view of student status remains delayed a full year. In Washington, in fact, community and technical college vocational directors identify this inherent delay as the most significant disadvantage involved in using such records. Using survey work, the alternative data collection method, many also entail significant delays because of workload and the need for multiple follow-ups.

This timing issue is important. Any snapshot of the employment status of former students must be sufficiently delayed to allow for a job search. It is unreasonable to expect that all graduates will be snapped up by the job market within a few months, especially in programs with a single annual graduation or infrequent licensing exam schedules. Linking to the October–December quarter is problematic in that earnings data in this period include end-of-year bonuses. Employment in this quarter may also capture atypical short-term seasonal work. Some occupations are cyclical in nature and the winter match may also be problematic. WSBCTC is now exploring the extent to which our winter employment snapshot distorts the actual employment status of construction program graduates. For this analysis, we are taking snapshots corresponding to each quarter in the year subsequent to spring graduation. In order to fully capture employment as former students enter and leave the work force, researchers should ideally match to four or five quarters after the students leave college, but this is costly and results in a data file substantially more complex than a single snapshot.

A final timing issue is that the UI wage file is structured by fiscal quarter. Academic records, in contrast, are structured by academic quarter or semester. Some of the linked data bases are also continuously updated. The researcher must make decisions about how to link these differently timed files for each employment status snapshot.

Issue of Uncovered Employment and Other Status. No administrative data bases track the people who opt out of the work force to engage in full-time homemaking or retirement. Similarly, unemployment is only partially tracked in administrative records. At the same time, UI wage files do not cover every job. Federal workers, for example, are not included in the state's UI file and self-employed workers may or may not be included, depending on whether they participate in the state's unemployment insurance system. Finally, the underground economy is exempt from any administrative recordkeeping at all. In Washington, we estimate that 85 percent of all wage and salary employment in the state is captured in the UI wage file. Florida reports that 97 percent of its workers are covered by the UI system (Pfeiffer, personal correspondence, May 1995). Although the fact that administrative records do not cover every aspect of our lives is reassuring to me as a citizen, as a researcher I find it most limiting.

States that regularly use UI wage files have a number of choices about how to address the issue of those not included in administrative records, and the method they use may affect the meaning of any reported employment rates. For example, I examined the choices made by Florida, North Carolina, Texas, and Washington. The impressively creative strategies used by each state result in quite different reported employment rates for graduates of two-year college vocational programs: 70, 96, 68, and 85 percent, respectively. However, these differences probably do not represent real variations in outcomes but result instead from the strategies each state uses to deal with the issue of those not covered in administrative records.

Strategies for addressing the uncovered status problem are of three basic kinds: report only the number and percentage in covered employment (as in Florida and Texas), create an employed-to-labor-force ratio, using the UI wage and benefit files and job service files (as in North Carolina), or find a way to estimate the status of those not covered by administrative records (as in Washington). Under the first method, states report employment status only for the universe of former students who are captured by the UI file and related administrative data bases—that is, those actually covered by the state's UI system. Because another 3–15 percent of students are employed but are not captured by the records of a given state, or are not in any administrative record, the covered employment rate is relatively low: 70 percent for two-year college vocational graduates in Florida (Pfeiffer, memo, January 1995). The 68 percent placement rate in Texas reflects the covered employment rate for two-year college vocational students in that state (Anderberg, 1994).

Turning to the second method, in some states it is possible to track most unemployed workers through administrative data bases. Those who receive unemployment benefits are present in a UI benefit history file in all states, but many unemployed people are not receiving benefits. In addition, some departments of labor or employment security operate a job placement service that captures individually identifiable information on a substantial portion of these unemployed workers—specifically, those who are looking for unskilled to midlevel work. Such is the case in North Carolina, where the Department of Community Colleges (NCDCC) uses the Job Service administrative file, combined with the UI benefit history and the UI wage file, to identify the number of students in the labor force. For accountability reporting, the NCDCC then creates an employment ratio by dividing the number employed by the number of former students who are linked in all three files. Because everyone who has opted out of the labor force is excluded from the divisor, the resulting employment ratio is a high 96 percent (Brown, 1994).

The third approach is to supplement administrative data links with other information to better describe the status of all students. In Washington, our strategy is to conduct an occasional survey on a statewide sample of former students not found in administrative records. We use the results of this survey to obtain information on students who cannot be found in administrative record files each year. To generate reports on the total number or percentage employed, going to college, or unemployed, WSBCTC adds these survey-based estimates for the unlinked students to the results of the administrative record link. This approach meets the data expectations of policy makers in my state who would immediately find the covered employment rate too low and the employment ratio too high.

Our estimates in Washington were based on a mailed survey to unlinked students. After six follow-ups, our initial mailed survey to the unlinked sample yielded a 54 percent response for the 85 percent of records with usable addresses. Adjusting the results for apparent response bias, we concluded that 58 percent of unlinked graduates were employed in the first calendar quarter of the year after leaving the college. The status of the other unlinked graduates was as follows: 14 percent students, 10 percent homemakers, 7 percent unemployed and seeking work, 6 percent discouraged workers not seeking work, 3 percent retired, and 2 percent disabled and not seeking work (Washington State Board for Community and Technical Colleges, 1993). These findings now serve as multipliers for the unlinked counts. We plan to update these multipliers by repeating the sample survey about every five years.

A final coverage issue arises when students do not supply their SSNs to the registrar at their institutions. Data links on name alone, or on name and date of birth, are cumbersome and require considerable manual intervention. We have found it best to rely on the SSN for administrative data links, leaving those without valid numbers unlinked. In Washington, only about 2 percent of those who leave vocational programs, including international students and recent immigrants, do not have a valid SSN. We exclude them from the files submitted for linking, and given the small number excluded, we make no adjustments in our outcomes reports for those excluded. FETPIP in Florida compares the name, birth date, and Social Security records for the same individual submitted by different agencies. FETPIP then eliminates mismatched records from all files. States with high immigrant enrollments may find that their number of students without valid SSNs is higher than in Washington because immigrants may not immediately acquire an SSN.

In sum, the single most important decision to be made in using administrative records for accountability reporting is how to handle the status of those not included in administrative records. This decision may decisively affect reported statistics on employment status. If no adjustment is made for the unlinked students, the advantage of eliminating survey response bias may be lost in light of the disadvantage of the noncoverage bias. For studies involving comparisons of pre- and post-training wages, on the other hand, the issue of the unlinked is of little concern because the UI wage file alone is adequate to calculate valid statistics.

Issues Related to the Confidentiality of Individually Identifiable Records. Federal Bureau of Labor Statistics confidentiality requirements, Department of Labor regulations, and state laws set the stage for confidentiality concerns related to use of UI wage records for data linking. Given the growing prominence of these uses for accountability purposes, confidentiality issues are a hot topic at the moment and are likely to have changed as this volume goes to press. It is important for educational researchers to acquaint themselves with the legal and ethical issues that are unique to the UI wage file and thus different from data-sharing among colleges, which is also governed by state law and, at the federal level, by the Family Educational Rights and Privacy Act of 1974 and the Buckley Amendment.

As with individual student data, it is important not to disclose information about an individual worker or business. To preclude inadvertent disclosure of a firm's identity, our match file in Washington contains only an industry code, not the employer identifier. Consequently, we have only limited employer information—a three-digit Standard Industrial Code (SIC), a categorical establishment size, and a worksite identifier. Even these limited data allow identification of our state's largest employer, which would be an inappropriate use of the UI wage link file. Although some data users see the omission of the identity of a firm as a significant limitation of a record-linking follow-up methodology when compared to survey approaches, we have found that knowing only the industry in which a former student is employed is useful for monitoring and research purposes. Although we do not have access to the identity of a firm, our data provider checks to see whether the student worked in the same firm before or during college and records the findings in our file. These strategies compensate for some of the limits imposed by confidentiality requirements.

Duplicate Records. The traditional follow-up survey is based on an assumed model that education at a single institution is always the "treatment" and that job placement following training is an appropriate outcome measure. This linear pipeline from a single institution to a single job may apply for some people, but administrative records capture a reality that is much more complex. A particular student may well have two or more records in the UI wage file for a given quarter. He or she might have worked for one firm for a few weeks of the quarter and then switched to another, or might work simultaneously for two or more firms (dental hygiene students, for example, typically work for several dentists). The record number of employers obtained in our linking process was set by a dental hygiene student who worked for fourteen employers in a single quarter.

From a data-management point of view, these nonsingular occurrences can be thought of as duplicate records. In some cases, recording multiple status for a student is valuable; in other situations, such as reporting earnings, multiple records are not helpful. To report total earnings for a person, the general contractor must add the wages obtained from all employers. For purposes of reporting the student's industry, county of employment, and size of firm, WSBCTC uses a protocol that selects a primary employer based on the highest-paying job. The Florida FETPIP system keeps track of all employment for the person and can report the extent to which a former student has earnings from more than one employer in a given quarter.

Furthermore, at any point in time a given student may have more than one status (employed and attending college, for example). It is possible to record these multiple conditions. At WSBCTC, we opted for a priority system. If a graduate is employed, WSBCTC does not attempt to determine whether he or she is attending college as well. Only those who are not present in the UI files are linked to our postsecondary enrollment records to determine their college-going status.

Issues Related to Identifying Quality of Employment or Placement. Although most employers in midlevel occupations hire workers based on experience, attitude, and communication skills, not years of school completed or academic performance (National Center on the Educational Quality of the Workforce, 1995), the accountability reporting systems used by most states generally rest on the assumption that training is the key to employment. Recognizing that in the case of half the nation's jobs, employment can be had without postsecondary training, some accountability systems require additional indicators that suggest that students actually used the skills and abilities obtained from the training they received.

Following this logic, many states look to the UI wage link to provide indicators of high-quality or training-related employment. Those that use earnings as a measure of quality are somewhat satisfied with the results from the administrative link. With the exception of Alaska, where data on specific occupations is included in the UI wage record, states that attempt to determine training-related employment as an indicator of quality face considerable difficulty. Most UI wage files, or the related ES-202 file, contain only information about the industry of employment. Given the substantial interest in and, in some cases, state requirement to report the percent employed in training-related occupations, states that engage in a UI wage match have created various ways to work around this major limitation. These are essentially of two types: employer surveys and industry-to-educational-program crosswalks.

General contractors in Florida and Texas conduct periodic employer surveys to determine the occupation of the former student. The employer survey used in these states is also the source of additional information on employee worksite, which is available only in limited fashion in the UI wage file. To determine relatedness to training, the general contractor codes the various occupational titles supplied by each employer through the survey according to standard Occupational Employment Statistic (OES) classifications. OES codes can then be linked to the CIP code of the program the student attended in order to determine relatedness to training. As a result of data-sharing between Florida and Texas, as well as accumulating years of experience in using employer surveys, most of the job titles supplied by employers can now be coded electronically without manual intervention. An existing National Occupational Information Coordinating Committee (NOICC) OES to CIP crosswalk can also be used as a starting point for establishing relatedness, but the OES-to-CIP match is not straightforward. For a variety of reasons, the NOICC crosswalk must be modified to reflect special circumstances in each state. Florida is currently asking college staff to help with this modification to the national crosswalk. FETPIP has asked staff to rate various program-to-industry to occupation links on a scale of relatedness. The results will be used to match survey and linked file data on one hand to the CIP codes of former students on the other. Centralized state-level employer surveys reduce cost and can lead to high response rates. Texas reports returns from 85 percent of the employers surveyed. Still, this annual survey work substantially increases the cost of accountability reporting.

The industry-to-educational program crosswalk requires more of an analytical leap than the survey method. The link essentially indicates whether the student is working in an industry that is regarded as typically employing people who have the specific technical skills taught by the training program. For example, the hospital industry employs nurses. Graduates of nursing programs who are employed by hospitals are coded as being in an industry related to their training, even though they might be running the coffee shop at the hospital and not working as nurses. The process typically is based on the NOICC OES-to-CIP crosswalk, with adjustments made for the individual state. The other half of the process requires some kind of OES-to-SIC crosswalk. In Washington, our data provider uses the industry profiles created every three years through an industry-based OES survey.

In the mid 1980s, researchers pushed to have employers report the actual occupations of their workers so that relatedness to training could be measured using a CIP-to-OES or CIP-to-SOC crosswalk. In the past few years, however, researchers have re-examined the idea of burdening employers with a census of occupational titles and are also questioning the real benefits obtained from the considerable effort required to work around these limits (Stevens and Shi, 1995).

Because of the increasing fluidity of job requirements, the meaningfulness of the relatedness-to-training measure as a quality indicator is increasingly questioned. Our experience with the SIC-to-OES-to-CIP linking process has been mixed. At the system level, the results pass most tests of reliability. When I explore particular programs at individual colleges, however, the year-to-year variability is greater than should be expected. The SIC-to-OES-to-CIP approach is apparently sensitive to some factor other than program quality or changing labor force conditions. In all states that use the relatedness-to-training measure, moreover, a good deal of effort is needed to gather the data. It is appropriate to have a national conversation about the costs and benefits of this quality indicator, especially in light of the increasing availability of other quality indicators.

Issues Associated with Wages. The UI wage file provides quarterly earnings, but only Washington's file also includes the number of hours worked. Most other states ask employers to report the number of weeks worked during a quarter. This difference stems from the leeway given to states in setting their UI eligibility thresholds, and Washington's threshold is 680 reported hours of work; in most other states, the threshold includes some count of weeks worked. Unfortunately, thirteen weeks of quarterly earnings may be for full-time or part-time work and the wage record in all states except Washington provide no firm evidence of which is the case. Still, there is considerable potential for making sense out of the quarterly earnings from the UI wage file. Florida looks to the number of weeks worked and the earnings to make a judgment about whether the former student worked full- or part-time (Pfeiffer, personal correspondence, May 1995). Stevens (1993) used a similar approach to identify likely full-time workers based on typical salaries by industry. Stevens has also applied his approach to Washington data. The results are strikingly similar to our standard procedure of using wage data based on earnings divided by the actual number of reported hours worked.

A timing issue is also associated with earnings data. Most states require reporting at the time of compensation. Earnings can increase and decrease simply because the number of paydays in each quarter can vary, especially with biweekly pay schedules or if bonus pay is involved. As noted earlier, this is particularly likely in the first and fourth quarters. It is also important to know that earnings for former students do not tend to be normally distributed. In my state, most vocational graduates work in entry-level jobs and earn wages between $5 and $14 an hour. Some earn $20 or more and none earn less than minimum wage. Given this skew in the distribution—typical of all earnings data—median earnings provide a better single measure of central tendency than using the mean. In Washington, the median hourly wage of graduates ($10 an hour in early 1994) is about $2 per hour lower than the mean. The choice of mean or median is therefore significant. Another alternative is to use categories rather than a single measure of central tendency. In recent publications, for example, I have reported the percentage of graduate earnings at various wage levels (under $6.50, $6.50 to under $10, $10 to under $15, and $15 and above).

Finally, when wages are compared from year to year, an inflation adjustment may be needed. Although the absolute median hourly earnings of graduates in Washington has risen over the last five years, the inflation-adjusted hourly wage remained stable until a recent economic downturn. At that point, the inflation-adjusted median hourly wage dropped by about $.20.

Job Mobility and Retention. Several state accountability systems require reporting on job retention, but few states have used the UI system for this purpose. Based on recent feedback from vocational administrators, WSBCTC links the same cohort three times against the UI wage files to provide this job retention analysis. The first link occurs in the first calendar quarter of the year after students leave the college, the second follows a year later, and the third a year after that. Analysis of the first two links shows increased employment rates at the second link, although some of those who were employed in the first link were receiving UI benefits by the time of the second link. North Carolina looks at the retention issues by linking to five successive quarters after enrollment.

Quality-of-employment issues, like the noncoverage issue, are ripe for nationwide dialogue. The work of David Stevens (1994, 1995) in exploring alternatives to the traditional employment rate and relatedness-to-training indicator is must reading for those developing work-related institutional or system indicators.

Providing Useful Information from Administrative Data Matches

Although Washington has been using the UI data link process since 1989, WSBCTC has only recently developed useful ways to share the findings with the faculty and staff responsible for program decisions. Initially, our goal was to conduct outcomes research, and findings were published in a research report. In the last few years, administrators and faculty have increasingly wanted outcomes data on their programs to aid in local decision making, and they see the UI link data as a valid and reliable source. Because of its summative and aggregate nature, however, the initial research report and subsequent annual reports of employment rates have not met their needs.

Recently WSBCTC conducted interviews with college staff to gather their opinions about how to make the UI link data more useful. The overwhelming request was for hands-on access to the data base. Staff want to be able to use the file directly to explore and answer questions as they arise. FETPIP staff in

Florida report a similar demand for hands-on access. New, inexpensive, user-friendly statistical software such as Survey by RaoSoft, Inc. can facilitate hands-on access to linked data. Such broad access to linked data requires special attention to issues of confidentiality.

Our interviews surfaced another barrier to use of administrative record matches. Some staff fear that using data of this kind summatively could place their programs in jeopardy. These fears are often expressed indirectly. For instance, questions are often raised about the many assumptions and trade-offs researchers must make when using administrative records. The reliability of relatedness-to-training measures often comes under question. The Texas general contractor addresses this issue in its publications by providing a step-by-step approach to using and interpreting the data (Anderberg, 1994).

Conclusions

Today, UI wage files and related data bases are being used effectively for accountability reporting and research. These files provide low-cost, high-quality data on the workplace status of former students. However, effective use of these data files requires a re-examination of many assumptions about the connection between education and work. Among them are the linear nature of this relationship and the degree to which any degree of relatedness can really be established given increasing job mobility and the rapidly changing nature of workplace skills. It also requires a flexible attitude and a willingness to select alternative strategies when administrative records fail to meet the researcher's exacting needs. All researchers would benefit from further national dialogue on issues of noncoverage and how to develop better indicators of quality training.

References

Anderberg, M. *Automated Student and Adult Learner Follow-up System, Final Report for Program Year 1993–94.* Austin: Texas State Occupational Information Coordinating Committee, 1994.

Brown, K. *1994 Critical Success Factors for the North Carolina Community College System, Fifth Annual Report.* Raleigh: North Carolina Department of Community Colleges, Planning and Research Section, 1994.

National Center on the Educational Quality of the Workforce. "First Findings from the EQW National Employer Survey." In *EQW Results.* Philadelphia: University of Pennsylvania, 1995.

Pfeiffer, J. J. "Student Follow-up Using Automated Record Linkage Techniques: Lessons From Florida's Education and Training Placement Information Program (FETPIP)." *Journal of Vocational Education Research,* 1995, *19* (3).

Stevens, D. W. *The School to Work Transition of High School and Community College Vocational Program Completers: 1990–1992* (EQW Working Paper 27). Philadelphia: National Center on the Educational Quality of the Workforce, University of Pennsylvania, 1993.

Stevens, D. W. *The Economic Value of the University of Maryland System to the State of Maryland.* Adelphi: University of Maryland System Administration, 1994.

Stevens, D. W. "Performance Measurement Revisited." *Journal of Vocational Education Research,* 1995, *19* (3).

Stevens, D. W., and Shi, J. *New Perspectives on Documenting Employment and Earnings Outcomes in Vocational Education.* Berkeley, Calif.: National Center for Research in Vocational Education, 1995.

Washington State Board for Community and Technical Colleges. "Adjusting Vocational Outcome Student Follow-up Data to Account for 'Unmatched' Students" (Technical Report 92–1). Olympia, Wash.: Washington State Board for Community and Technical Colleges, 1993.

LORETTA J. SEPPANEN is manager for research and analysis for the Washington State Board for Community and Technical Colleges.

As they harness student tracking's new technical possibilities, institutional researchers should remain aware of time-honored design principles for conducting longitudinal studies.

Some Concluding Thoughts

Peter T. Ewell

As the preceding chapters suggest, student tracking's new frontiers are indeed wide and growing. Institutional researchers entering this territory for the first time will find that it contains far richer resources than those available to their counterparts of a generation ago. But they may also find useful some advice drawn from the experiences of these early pioneers and verified repeatedly with each technical advance. These lessons can be conveniently grouped under two main headings: issues associated with longitudinal data base design and those surrounding analysis and reporting.

Design Issues

Changes affecting data base design include vast increases in the number and contents of data sources available to support longitudinal studies (both within and outside a given institution) and major gains in the flexibility with which appropriate data files can be assembled. Although both advances increase analytical scope and power, they also add immeasurably to complexity. Researchers now have hundreds of data elements at their disposal as potential candidates for inclusion in a particular dataset. In fact, so many are available that exercise of the traditional default option—including everything in the hope that it might come in handy—simply entails too much overhead. More powerful data-manipulation tools now enable researchers to easily escape the rigidity associated with using traditional longitudinal cohort data structures. However, these new tools allow so many alternative ways to reassemble this vastly increased array of potential data elements that analytical consistency may be threatened. Given this emerging complexity, some old lessons of tracking system design may be helpful.

Think Comprehensively. Far too many longitudinal data structures are developed piecemeal in response to the demands of the moment. As illustrated by the evolution of federal Student Right-to-Know reporting requirements, external demands for statistics such as graduation and persistence rates are often maddeningly inconsistent, requiring information on differently defined populations and using different operational measures of the same underlying concept. As many of the chapters in this volume illustrate, flexible analytical and data-assembly tools now allow such demands to be met far more quickly than they used to be. The temptation to take each such request as it comes, and to conduct a wholly independent analysis in response, should be resisted. Some data elements will apply to virtually all student populations and really are of more importance for tracking than others. These should be carefully identified up front, their definitional integrity ensured, and clearly marked paths established through documentation to access them on a regular basis. At the same time, the creation of isolated special-purpose datasets assembled solely to keep track of particular student populations should be avoided. To ensure consistency, studies of such populations should instead begin with a core dataset; students who meet the required population characteristics to be included in the study should be identified and extracted from that dataset and, if needed, additional data elements specific to that population merged into the resulting analytic file at a later point.

An Analytic System Is Not an Operational System. As tracking capabilities have advanced, equally dramatic progress has occurred in the basic operational data systems supporting such institutional recordkeeping functions as registration and admissions. Of course, these are the systems that contain most of the data elements on which tracking depends. More specifically, such recordkeeping systems are far more real-time in nature and relational in structure than ever before. In the light of these developments, it has become popular to claim that the kinds of derived analytic data bases described in this volume are not really needed: having complete student histories on-line in the registration system in a fully relational data structure should automatically allow tracking to occur. Experience so far suggests the opposite. Indeed, the more an operational records system is optimized to retrieve and display real-time data about particular students—to support an individual intervention or an advising session, for example—the less likely it has proven to be capable of generating the kind of point-in-time information about groups of students needed for consistent analysis. At least as important, the proprietary software typically associated with such systems rarely allows easy data extraction or enables the user to incorporate data drawn from outside the institution (such as that noted in Chapters Four, Six, and Seven of this volume) in an analysis. For the institutional researcher, therefore, the construction of derived data bases—carefully designed to support longitudinal analyses—remains as important as ever. What's different now, as Victor Borden reminds us in Chapter Five, is that derived point-in-time files now come in many varieties and can be combined quickly and flexibly to address quite different analytical questions. The researcher need not be wedded, as in the past, to a single longitudinal cohort structure.

Capture Is Everything. Increased flexibility of this kind, however, puts an even greater premium on planning and documenting the kinds of data capture or extraction procedures used to assemble regularly used analytic files. As emphasized in Chapter Five, managing the timing of any extraction is a critical issue. All public and most private institutions already have conventions in place for freezing student data at a defined census date, but other important points in time may be considerably less clearly or consistently defined. For instance, what constitutes the actual end of a given academic term: a particular date on the academic calendar, the time at which grades are actually turned in, the time at which students are officially cleared to graduate, or the time by which all relevant data related to the term's activity are ultimately keyed into the institution's registration system? As any practicing institutional researcher knows, these dates may be separated by months, and a lot can happen in between. As the flexible use of discrete point-in-time extracts becomes more common, not only must they be accomplished consistently, but all users of the resulting data also need to be aware of the analytical consequences of any particular timing.

This leads to a more general issue because the derived data files typically used for institutional research purposes on most campuses remain notoriously undocumented. As long as this array consisted of only a few commonly structured data bases used inside an institutional research shop, this phenomenon did not constitute a major problem (although it was still bad practice). As users acquire greater access to such files and can combine them in increasingly flexible ways—as in a data warehouse environment—it is imperative that adequate definitions be provided for all data elements included in such files, as well as appropriate documentation as to when and how data capture occurs.

Analytic and Presentational Issues

The results of longitudinal studies have always been unusually difficult to communicate to lay audiences. Part of this problem is attributable to the conceptual core of such studies—the notion of a tracking cohort—does not correspond to any of the familiar and recognizable groups of students (such as first-year students or business majors) with whom administrators are accustomed to dealing. More importantly, longitudinal studies can get very complicated very fast, as both the variety of groups to be tracked and the variables included in any analysis proliferate. Once again, some old rules may be helpful:

Model It First. Above all, student tracking is about documenting the many paths students may choose in the course of an educational career—either inside or beyond a particular institution—and determining the specific consequences of the choices they make. This essential directionality means that it is often helpful to explicitly map out a particular set of presumed events or hypotheses before attempting an analysis. Physically drawing a simple conceptual model that illustrates the many ways in which a particular student might act out a potential sequence of experiences and choices, and specifying the kinds of outcomes that might result at each point, remains a helpful exercise before beginning any longitudinal study. Modeling of this kind becomes especially important when large numbers of variables will be included in the analysis and when the values of these variables are time-dependent or depend on a particular sequence of prior events or conditions.

Think in Layers. With respect to enrollment behavior (or anything else for that matter), few colleges or universities enroll a homogeneous student population. Most instead serve multiple and distinct student clienteles, each of which can be described in terms of specific clusters of cross-cutting descriptive or behavioral characteristics (such as traditionally aged, first-time-in-college, day-attending students). Moreover, these populations may experience very different patterns of enrollment over time. Given such diversity, observed variations in institutional performance on such measures as persistence or degree completion—either among institutions or for a single institution over time—are far more likely to be due to variations in the student clientele mix than they are the result of real differences in institutional performance.

In this light, appropriate disaggregation becomes the heart of any analysis. The most effective data analysis and presentation strategies begin with an institutional bottom line on a set of easily understood performance measures (such as degree completion, fall-to-fall re-enrollment, or successful completion of a college-level math course), then successively disaggregate results for particular subpopulations. Rarely are bivariate presentations sufficient under these conditions, and the best analyses may be based on several such layers of successive disaggregation. Often, multivariate statistical techniques can help sort out this complexity, but because most decision makers find such approaches obscure, it is a good idea to present ultimate results in terms of the experiences of specific student groups, using multivariate techniques to identify the most powerful combinations of factors to use in defining the subpopulations to display.

Examine All the Alternatives. Considerable diversity among institutional environments and student clienteles also means that the same patterns may not be apparent everywhere. Just because the research literature, for example, points to an overall relationship between on-campus residence and first-year persistence does not mean that this is the case on any given campus or for particular subgroups of students. In fact, the most useful findings for policy often occur when a particular local population is discovered to be acting unexpectedly, either in the light of national trends or of institutional preconceptions. One of the most common preconceptions is that students are actually doing what we tell them to do. However, close examination of such matters as placement or course-taking behavior reveals surprising numbers of cases in which students, with or without official encouragement, are not following established institutional policies. Many of these deviations appear to have real impacts on performance. As a result, one of the most useful applications of student tracking methodologies is to determine whether such policies are producing the desired or expected behaviors.

Keep It Simple. Few admonitions to the institutional researcher are more common than this one, but it applies especially to communicating the results of longitudinal studies. Once an analysis is complete, it is crucial to determine what three or four salient points its results suggest and to take special pains to illustrate these points consistently. At the same time, because the experience of different student subpopulations may vary considerably from institutional averages, it is important for the researcher to head off any too general policy conclusions that might be drawn hastily from the findings presented. Again, carefully layered presentations that first provide institution-level results, and then show how these are made up of many different kinds of experiences with different policy consequences, are generally best. Patterns of student flow, success, and failure are also far better illustrated by pictures than by numbers or by words. A consistent set of graphics or flow diagrams should be used in every presentation.

Points such as these remind us that the essence of student tracking has not changed despite the considerable evolution of tools and available data sources described in this volume. As we enter a decade in which student educational career paths are likely to become more complex than ever, institutional researchers will be well-advised to remember the basics while exploiting these new technical possibilities.

PETER T. EWELL *is senior associate at the National Center for Higher Education Management Systems in Boulder, Colorado.*

ADDITIONAL RESOURCES

Although it covers much ground to explore the new frontiers of student tracking, this volume makes no pretense of mapping the territory. For those interested in taking next steps, a range of additional resources may be helpful. Several are listed and briefly described in this section, structured around major topics addressed in the volume.

Resources on Longitudinal Data Base Design

Standard published references on this topic include the following:

Ewell, P. T. "Principles of Longitudinal Enrollment Analysis: Conducting Retention and Student Flow Studies." In J. A. Muffo and G. W. McLaughlin (eds.), *A Primer on Institutional Research*. Tallahassee, Fla.: Association for Institutional Research, 1987, pp. 1–19.

Terenzini, P. T. "Student Attrition and Retention." In J. A. Muffo and G. W. McLaughlin (eds.), *A Primer on Institutional Research*. Tallahassee, Fla.: Association for Institutional Research, 1987, pp. 20–35.

These two chapters present basic principles for establishing data bases to investigate attrition/retention and student flow using institutional records information and survey-based panel methodologies, respectively. Together, they provide a good conceptual introduction to this topic for the newcomer.

Middaugh, M. F. "Persistence." In M. A. Whiteley, J. D. Porter, and R. H. Fenske (eds.), *The Primer for Institutional Research*. Tallahassee, Fla.: Association for Institutional Research, 1992, pp. 1–11.

This source provides a step-by-step approach to establishing a simple cohort tracking data base in a practical manner, again suited especially for newcomers to the topic.

Ewell, P. T., Parker, R. W., and Jones, D. P. *Establishing a Longitudinal Student Tracking System: An Implementation Handbook*. Boulder, Colo.: National Center for Higher Education Management Systems, 1988.

This is a comprehensive manual for establishing a tracking data base using the free-standing cohort methodology. It includes recommended data element descriptions and sample file and report layouts and is based on experience in establishing the multi-institutional LONESTAR student tracking consortium for two-year colleges in Texas.

Palmer, J. *Accountability Through Student Tracking: A Review of the Literature.* Washington, D.C.: American Association of Community and Junior Colleges, 1990.

Bers, T. H. (ed.). *Using Student Tracking Systems Effectively.* New Directions for Community Colleges, no. 66. San Francisco: Jossey-Bass, 1989.

The Palmer book reviews the extant literature on developing tracking systems in a two-year college context, including the calculation of appropriate indicators of effectiveness for discharging accountability to external bodies. The Bers article is also useful in this context.

Other resources available in this area include workshops on tracking system design offered regularly as Professional Development Workshops and as preconference sessions at the Association for Institutional Research (AIR) annual forum each spring (contact AIR, 314 Stone Building, Florida State University, Tallahassee, FL 32306-3038; phone 904-644-4470; e-mail air@mailer.fsu.edu). The National Center for Higher Education Management Systems (NCHEMS) also offers regular seminars on establishing student tracking systems as well as providing consulting on tracking system development and implementation. NCHEMS also writes such systems on contract in SPSS and SAS (contact NCHEMS, P.O. Drawer P, Boulder, CO 80301; phone 303-497-0301; e-mail nchems@spot.colorado.edu).

Organizations, Consortia, and Systems Developers

A number of institutional consortia and clearinghouses have been established to share data and approaches on topics related to retention and student tracking or to provide consulting services.

The LONESTAR Consortium. Founded by two-year colleges in Texas, the LONESTAR consortium maintains and shares common tracking software written in SPSS, holds conferences twice a year, and engages in other joint ventures. An updated version of this software (called LONESTAR+) is currently being written in FoxPro for use in a Windows environment. Although the majority of members of LONESTAR remain Texas community colleges, membership in the consortium can be negotiated for four-year institutions and for institutions from neighboring states (contact LONESTAR, Brazosport College, 500 College Drive, Lake Jackson, TX, 77566; phone 409-266-3000 ext. 260; e-mail rparker@brazospor.cc.tx.us).
The LARC Consortium. The Learning Assessment Retention Consortium (LARC) comprises two-year colleges in California and engages in joint research pro-

jects on topics related to retention and student outcomes (contact Rancho Santiago College Research Center, 17th at Bristol, Santa Ana, CA 92706; phone 714-667-3345).

The AASCU/Sallie Mae Retention Project. Housed at the American Association of State Colleges and Universities (AASCU), this project collects data on retention and graduation rates from over 350 four-year institutions, as well as disseminating information on best practices in campus-based retention programs (contact AASCU, One Dupont Circle, Washington, DC 20036-1192; phone 202-293-7070).

Consortium for Student Retention Data Exchange. Since 1994, the University of Oklahoma at Norman has operated a data-sharing service involving graduation and retention rates for baccalaureate-granting institutions. Participation is on a fee-for-service basis, with participating institutions providing their own data and receiving in return a set of standard comparative reports based on peer institutions included in the consortium (contact Office of Institutional Research, University of Oklahoma-Norman, 660 Parrington Oval, Norman, OK 73019; phone 405-325-3681; e-mail wa0486@uokmvsa).

Noel/Levitz, Inc. Founded by two former retention researchers, this consulting firm currently offers training in establishing retention data-collection and intervention systems. Noel/Levitz currently hosts a national conference on student retention, offers a seminar series, and produces and markets PC-based software (*ActionTrack* and *Dialogue*) designed to track high-risk students and manage effective interventions by campus offices (contact Noel/Levitz Centers, Inc., 902 East Second Ave., Coralville, IA 52241; phone 800-728-4700).

Data-Linking for Purposes of Follow-up

Effective use of state-level unit-record information and UI wage-record linkages for purposes of follow-up tracking is still evolving, and more definitive sources will probably be available in the future. At this point, the best resources for each major type of data included under this heading are the following.

State-Level Enrollment Data. The State Higher Education Executive Officers organization (SHEEO) in Denver has a standing contract with the National Center for Education Statistics (NCES) of the U.S. Department of Education to coordinate state-level data reporting. Because of the growing salience of state-level unit-record data systems as resources for accountability reporting, the effective use of such records to calculate graduation rates and track interinstitutional enrollment flow has become a prominent topic for this organization. The SHEEO/NCES project holds an annual data conference each summer, conducts periodic surveys of state capabilities, and generally tracks topics related to statewide data collection and use (contact SHEEO/NCES Communication Network, 707 17th Street, Suite 2700, Denver, CO 80202-3427; phone 303-299-3685; e-mail arussell@ecs.org). Although some states (such as Illinois) maintain free-standing consortia to provide access to information about subsequent enrollment, the SHEEO organization in each state is the best place to start for any given institutional researcher seeking information about such data sources.

Electronic Transcript Exchange. The Committee on the Standardization of Postsecondary Education Electronic Data Exchange of the American Association of Collegiate Registrars and Admissions Officers (AACRAO) together with the Exchange of Permanent Records Electronically for Students and Schools project of the Council of Chief State School Officers at the NCES have been engaged in a long-standing joint project to develop standard codes and formats for the electronic exchange of transcript information among educational institutions at all levels. To date, *Data Element Dictionaries* and basic transaction sets have been developed for most major student-related functions, and have received certification as an international data standard by the American National Standards Institute. These codes and formats are intended for use by all institutions wishing to exchange such information (contact AACRAO, One Dupont Circle NW, Suite 330, Washington, DC 20036-1171; phone 202-293-9161; e-mail becraftw@aacrao.nche.edu).

Administrative Data Bases/School-to-Work Transitions. Established at the University of Baltimore to conduct research on the effectiveness of vocational education, the Jacob France Center generally has the latest and most comprehensive national information about techniques for linking administrative records (such as UI wage records) for research purposes (contact The Jacob France Center, Merrick School of Business, University of Baltimore, 1420 North Charles St., Baltimore, MD 21201-4729; phone 410-837-4729). Center staff have also collaborated on a reference work in this area: D. W. Stevens and J. Shi's *New Perspectives on Documenting Employment and Earnings Outcomes in Vocational Education* (Berkeley, Calif.: National Center for Research in Vocational Education, 1995).

Another helpful reference is K. A. Levesque and M. N. Alt, *A Comprehensive Guide to Using Unemployment Insurance Data for Program Follow-Up* (Berkeley, Calif.: Institute for the Study of Family, Work and Community, 1995).

In each state, an excellent and often-underused resource in this area is its State Occupational Information Coordinating Committee (SOICC). SOICCs typically conduct labor studies that link training with work force placement, and their data people generally are among the most knowledgeable in a given state about how to handle electronic data linkages involving administrative records. Most have also developed appropriate crosswalks between educational programs and occupational titles or industry classifications that can be used to help determine appropriate job placement.

INDEX